The Music of His Promises

∞

The Music of His Promises

Listening to God With
Love, Trust, and Obedience

Elisabeth Elliot

SERVANT PUBLICATIONS
ANN ARBOR, MICHIGAN

Vine books is an imprint of Servant Publications especially designed to serve
evangelical Christians.

Published by Servant Publications
P.O. Box 8617
Ann Arbor, Michigan 48107

Cover design: David Uttley Design

01 02 03   10 9 8 7 6 5

Printed in the United States of America
ISBN 1-56955-216-9

Cataloging-in-Publication Data on file at the Library of Congress.

The Music of His Promises

On dark days when the only song we feel like singing is a dirge, we can pray, "Let the music of thy promises be on my tongue" (Ps. 119:172). This is no tear-jerking ballad of how I'm feeling. The promises of God will lift me right out of sad sentimentality and put music in my mouth if I will think steadily on them. Here's one to sing: "Unfailing love enfolds him who trusts in the Lord" (Ps. 32:10).

Do you *feel* nothing of the kind? When did the validity of the Eternal Word rest on the mood of one of His poor children?

Let the promise be the song you sing. He will hear it and make it true for *you*.

At Every Stage of the Journey

What matters in life is that we should stick with the Lord. Where He goes, we follow. When He says halt, we halt. This is how it was with Israel—as He led them all those years in the wilderness of their journey to the Promised Land, they moved when the pillar of cloud and fire moved, and they camped when it stood still. The most amazing thing about that story is the most amazing thing about ours—*the Lord of Hosts is with us!* The pillar of cloud, visible by day, had fire in it at night, so "the Israelites could see it at every stage of their journey" (Exod. 40:38).

Some stops of our wilderness saga seem very difficult and very lonely. We look in vain for any indication around us that the presence of the Lord is still there. Where has He gone? Did we miss the way? Has He forgotten to be gracious? There is no "pillar" for us. But oh yes, there is—it is His unbreakable Word. Hold on to that. Count on it. Believe it. That is our pillar of the proof of His presence: "Be assured, I am with you always, to the end of time" (Matt. 28:20)

That promise, like the wonderful cloud with fire in it, is for every stage of our journey. That means *today*.

The Eye of the Needle

A husband and wife came seeking counsel for their marriage. As they told their story, fear and pride were revealed as the root causes of strife. The healing of that fear and the renunciation of that pride seemed utter impossibilities— just as impossible as for a rich man to enter the Kingdom of heaven, weighed down as he is with much baggage. This man and woman are weighed down too, yet wanting very much to rescue their home, to do God's will, to enter the Kingdom. It is, quite simply, impossible—"with men." But it is possible with God. He who calls us higher, beckons us in the direction of holiness and joy, is able to restore us, able to save, able to do more than we can ask or think, able to make even a camel go through the eye of a needle.

Recognition

T he temptation comes at us daily in some form or other to stand on our so-called rights, to desire to be appreciated for what we think we are, and to be given our "proper" place. This was what the mother of James and John was looking for—not for herself, but (for a mother this comes to almost the same thing) for her sons. She asked Jesus to assign them seats in heaven (see Matt. 20). Jesus answered that the privilege was not His to grant. He used the incident to teach the lesson we need every day: don't bother about making the weight of your "authority" felt. Forget about "who you are." Don't give a moment's thought to *rights* if you are in earnest about following *Me*, for I am the one, remember, who came to serve and to *give up*—not only My position with the Father, not only all My "rights" and My very glory, but My life. Do you feel you deserve to be first? Be a servant. Give up everything. Together, then, we will enter into joy!

Give and Give and Give

H aving been asked to speak to a group of ministers' wives, I asked the young wife of a minister what she would want to say to them. Many young people nowadays, I said, have grown up without any idea of hardship or sacrifice, and when it is required of them in the Lord's service, they rebel.

"Tell them to give and give and give, not expecting anything in return," the young woman said.

"But what if they say 'I'm having a really hard time with this. I'm struggling, I'm not really sure I can *do* that?'"

"Tell them 'I can do all things through Christ who strengtheneth me.'"

It was a clear word, spoken with the conviction of obedience. This young woman knows the struggle. She has experienced rejection and ingratitude. But she knows the truth of God's promise of strength.

The Way Appointed

It was at the supper with Jesus' disciples, on the night before He was crucified, that He told them He was going "the way appointed." That meant betrayal, by one of the very men sharing the same meal with Him, and crucifixion, at the hands of others who had arranged to pay this man. Yet in and through those terrible things that were to happen to Him, Jesus never for a moment thought of Himself as solely in their hands, at their mercy. He was held in the will of the Father. There was sovereign purpose in it all; the way He must travel was no accident of fate. It was *appointed*, assigned, a date with destiny. He accepted it as such.

What agonies we would spare ourselves if we would remember that ours, too, is a way appointed. We need not ever imagine that our circumstances are in any other hands than those that held the beloved Son obedient unto death.

What Is Trust?

To the unbeliever, the notion of "trust" in God is a challenge to *Him* to grant what one wants. When Jesus hung nailed to the cross, passersby hurled abuse at Him: "Come down. Save yourself!" The chief priests, lawyers and elders (learned, logical leaders) mocked Him: "King of Israel, indeed! Let Him come down now from the cross and then we will believe Him. Did He trust in God? Let God rescue Him." (Matt. 27:42-43).

Real trust yields utterly to the one trusted. All desire is turned over to that one, believing his ability to manage, control, and finally to accomplish what is best. When we pray, we should beware lest we line ourselves up with the mockers of Jesus—"If *You* do such and such, then I will trust You!" We need to learn rather to let God rescue us in His own way. It may not be escape from suffering, but death—followed by so much more glorious a rescue—*resurrection!*

Lord, teach me this trust.

Unimaginable Solutions

Spectators at the cross of Calvary imagined a dramatic escape or rescue as the proof of Jesus' kingship. God had an infinitely greater demonstration in mind. The Son would not manage to escape from the hands of His captors or from the nails and wood that held Him, nor would someone else come to His rescue. He would go through the last extremity of what it means to be human, and *by that very means,* by death itself, He *would destroy* the power of death. He would become, by His obedient dying, the "Death of Death" and "Hell's Destruction."

When we, in our "lesser miseries," plead for escape or rescue, what unimaginable "solutions" God has stored up for us! But often, in response to our pleadings, the word is Trust Me.

Looking at Graves

Matthew tells us in the last chapter of his Gospel that the two Marys came early in the morning, "to look at the grave." We can picture the sorrowful scene—two women in the gray dawn standing helplessly, contemplating the tomb. There was nothing left to hope for, nothing to see but a rock. We can see their drawn faces, bowed heads, the sag of their shoulders. Can we possibly picture those faces when there came a sudden earthquake, the descent of an angel, and the stone was rolled away from the grave? The angel was so dazzling, the guards (tough men, surly, and not in the least sorrowing like the women) collapsed in terror. The angel addressed the women: "You ... have nothing to fear.... He has been raised ..." (Matt. 28:5, 7). A few minutes later Jesus suddenly stood in their path.

We sometimes find ourselves looking at a "grave"—the end of all our hopes. We are helpless, defeated. Our faces are long, our shoulders droop. What a difference it would make then if, *by faith*, we would lift up our eyes to see the bright angel and the risen Savior. We really have nothing to fear—He has risen, exactly as He said. What a defeat His crucifixion seemed. What a triumph His resurrection was—and *is*, forever.

Don't look at the grave. Look up. Jesus stands risen beside you, alive forever! Then think of His comforting word: "And be assured, I am with you always, to the end of time" (Matt. 28:20).

Too Rich to Follow Him

I n the forests of Ecuador I soon learned that there were journeys I could not make if I wanted to carry baggage. Traveling narrow, muddy, and often steep trails on foot was impossible if I was heavily loaded.

So it is with the spiritual journey. We cannot make it if we insist on taking along everything we think indispensable. A rich young man was attracted to Jesus and contemplated joining His company, but Jesus spoke plainly of the necessary condition: Sell all you have first.

If he had not had much, perhaps he would have laid it down readily. But he was too rich to follow Jesus. He turned away, sorrowful.

We may be willing to part with *almost* everything God is asking us to relinquish, but perhaps we are clutching one thing tightly—"all but this, Lord." "Lay it down," Jesus says. "Let it go." If we refuse, too rich to follow Him, we have chosen a greater poverty in the end.

Too Strong to Be Crucified

Jesus Christ, we are told, was "crucified in weakness." When we approach the table of the Lord in Holy Communion, or when in any way at all we identify ourselves as Christians, we are letting Christ take us, with our purposes, and offer us, as He did His own body, up to His Father.

The greater our consciousness of weakness, sinfulness, and abject need, the more perfectly we can let Christ take us for that offering.

The man or woman who claims some autonomy, some right to himself, some independence, some existence of his own, is too strong. Too strong to need a Savior, too strong to flee to His cross for refuge, too strong to be crucified with Christ. How then shall he live in Christ, how shall Christ live in him?

> When I survey the wondrous Cross
> On which the Prince of Glory died,
> My richest gain I count but loss,
> And pour contempt on all my pride.

Isaac Watts

Too Proud for the Low Gate

If it is our habit to demand of God answers, solutions, explanations, we may find ourselves traveling a broad intellectual highway that leads to destruction. If it is really life we want, we must accept the narrow way and the very low gate. The questions, the problems not solved, the mystery not explained will be for the one who would press on to know the Lord. He is called by a still, small voice to humility and poverty of spirit—only by that road will he be allowed to see God. He must believe Him even when carrying in his heart the unanswered question. The problem he desperately wants solved is God's means of getting his attention—not necessarily that He may reveal its solutions but most certainly that He may reveal *Himself* to him. But let him not forget—it is the pure in heart who see God (see Matt. 5:8).

Too Busy to Be Quiet

If we are bent on a mad tear through life, God will allow us that liberty, but He will not tear madly about with us. He will wait for us until we quiet down and wait on Him. Sometimes we are not interested in quietness until things have suddenly fallen apart or come to a screeching halt, and then, in the ensuing silence we know that we cannot cure our evils and neither is God going to cure them. What He has been waiting for is our attention, our eyes turned to Him who is the very Life of All the Ages, the Light that our darkness can never overcome, Christ Himself, with us, in us, suffering, loving, and transforming us into the same image.

No Wagons Provided

For the transportation of the tabernacle in Old Testament times wagons and oxen were provided, to the Gershonites and the Merarites. But Moses gave none to the Kohathites, "because the service laid upon them was that of the holy things: these they had to carry themselves on their shoulders" (Num. 7:9).

It is well to remember that economy and efficiency are not necessarily important to God. We can hardly think in any other terms. "Get the job done with as little effort as possible. Don't strain yourself!" Some jobs, it seems, require individual sacrifice. It is not because they are of less value to God that He does not provide "wagons" (any modern methods or means to facilitate things) but because the job is *specially* important. He wants people. He wants consecration. He wants shoulders willing to bend.

Power and Love

The most powerful people are not often the most loving, and the most loving people often seem quite powerless in human terms. When the great question is raised: Why does God permit suffering? It is answered by some that He is powerless to prevent it, even though He may love us, and by others that He cannot possibly be loving, for surely He does have the power to prevent evil.

When Lazarus died the crowd of mourners was divided when Jesus wept. Some took it as evidence of how greatly He had loved the man. Others thought it a hypocritical gesture, since one who could heal a blind man certainly could have prevented this man's death.

Jesus did indeed love Lazarus, and Mary and Martha. He could have prevented his death. But certain things, in a broken world, must be allowed to happen. None of them, however, in the hands of a loving and powerful God and Savior, are beyond redeeming. Resurrection is a far greater evidence of the power and the love of God than the mere aborting of catastrophies. God, help us to remember this triumphant hope when we, too, stand weeping hopelessly.

More Toward the Light

L ast night I talked with a woman in trouble. Her troubles are complex, but there is one simple thing she could do. She simply doesn't want to do it.

This morning I flew out of Boston's Logan International Airport. As often, the airport was shrouded in fog which rolls in from the sea. The plane rose quickly from the dim, wet runway, passed through thick clouds to thin, and suddenly was in sunshine, with brilliant blue sky above, and all the clouds and fog far below. The plane had moved toward the light.

Christ is the Light of the World. His truth shines like the sun. But we must adore Him. We must learn to move in the direction of the light, no matter how dim and obscure the situation in which we find ourselves. If I adore Him who is all light, in whom "there is no darkness at all" (1 John 1:5), then darkness (even the least shading of the truth) will be intolerable to me.

Lord, how often I prefer the fog! I am preoccupied with my troubles when I could be occupied with adoration—moving up into His sunshine.

Our Daily Bread

We are used to praying "Give us today our daily bread" (Matt. 6:11) but we are not used to recognizing the answer and giving thanks for it. Most of us say grace at the table, perhaps, but daily bread includes all that we really need in this world. Do we believe God can and does provide that? Or are we like the Israelites who, when a "mixed company of strangers" came along, developed a whole new set of expectations? They were "greedy for better things" (Num. 11:4).

Sometimes God wants to give us better things. Those who really have trusted Him receive His gifts with thanksgiving. The spirit of greed is not in them. Rather they ask for and accept "daily" bread—in abundance, if God sees that to be good for them, or in sufficiency alone, according to His loving-kindness.

Help me, Lord, to take today's portion of food, possessions, joys, pain, and Your presence, believing that it is enough for me.

False Conclusions

When the children of Israel received the report of the tall men of Eshcol they were terrified, they refused to go up, and immediately concluded that God hated them. How could He love them if He had taken them out of Egypt only to deliver them over to giants to be wiped out? (See Deut. 1:27.)

It looked like a logical deduction, based on what little human evidence they had. But of course they were totally ignoring far more important and trustworthy evidence: the promises of God. He had promised a rich land, a Father's care, and everything they would need en route.

We look backwards at the "good old days," and bemoan our losses; we look around us to the many threats to our security, and tremble with fear. Our conclusions are false. God has not forgotten us, He does not hate us. He is taking us to a rich land if we will only trust and obey instead of making things complicated for ourselves.

Bearing Others' Burdens

M oses was appointed to carry the load of spiritual responsibility for God's chosen people. It was a heavy burden, and one for which he needed the help of God and of other men, but he sinned as the Israelites did and was denied the privilege of going into the Promised Land. One who is given the task of leadership must be prepared to be identified with those he leads, even to suffer punishment with them. Moses pled with God for permission to cross over and see the rich land promised to them, "but because of you," he said to Israel, "the Lord brushed me aside and would not listen." He answered, "Say no more about this ... give Joshua his commission, encourage and strengthen him, for he will lead this people across" (Deut. 3:27-28). Moses was a truly *meek* man—not by any means weak, but strong in God's strength. He was not offended. He accepted the verdict, and obeyed. It took a real man to commission, encourage, and strengthen another to do the job he had so longed to bring to completion.

The Rejection of Sacrifice

Obedience to God very often appears to us, at first glance, to mean sacrifice. We shrink from it. Sacrifice always involves death, and we reject death. But the divine paradox, the one we find running throughout all of Scripture, is that this sacrifice—the offering of ourselves in obedience to God— always means *life*. It is life, nothing less than life, that God offers us, so when we disobey, what we are actually doing is choosing death.

"The Lord commanded us to observe all these statutes and to fear the Lord our God; it will be for our own good at all times, and he will continue to preserve our lives" (Deut. 6:24).

We balk at something our conscience tells us we must do— "I don't see how *that* could be for my 'good,'"—but God does not discuss with us the how or the why. He simply makes clear *what* it is we must do. Then we must take His word for it that it will mean life to us. Every day He sets two things before us—life and death. Every day we choose sacrifice, which leads to life, or selfishness, the rejection of sacrifice, which leads to death. We can count on it, for we have the Word of the Lord that it is so.

Unconditional Self-Abandonment

The glory of the Resurrection followed the shame of the Crucifixion. Christ abandoned Himself, became subject to death, went to Gehenna, for love of us. Therefore He was raised in power, death could not hold Him, and He opened Paradise for us. We can enter only as He entered—the road to glory is always the road of self-abandonment. When we see this as a mere theory we are not even close to living as Christians. It is in the opportunities of every day, with real people (i.e., real sinners) that we (sinners, too) are called to His companionship: "Give up your rights, abandon yourself, follow me—follow me to the place where death cannot possibly hold you, where animosities and offenses are vanquished, and Life springs victorious."

What do we long for above all else? Is it not Life? Jesus came so that we could have it—but the only life He can give us is resurrection life. That kind comes as the result of unconditional self-abandonment.

Life and Peace

To most of us, I suppose, life and peace are the two most precious things, for without them the love of friends and family, the pleasures of God's world, the possessions we have been given, cannot be enjoyed. Life, in the spiritual sense, is given in exchange for selfishness. Peace also is given when we stop doing only what we please. It never *seems* possible that life and peace will be ours if we let go—the enemy sees to that, relentlessly trying to persuade us how necessary it is to hang onto our rights, to keep control. Have we ever, even once in our lives, found deep and lasting peace by that method?

God draws us always *away* from "Egypt," land of bondage, of self-will, and idolatry, to what He calls "a place of rest."

"You shall not act as we act here today," Moses told Israel, "each of us doing what he pleases, for till now you have not reached the place of rest" (Deut. 12:8).

The Price of Life

He saved others, but he cannot save Himself" (Matt. 27:42). This was a joke among the chief priests and lawyers. If they had comprehended the profound truth of their jest it would have died on their lips. If He had saved Himself He would have saved no one else. The principle is true for us as well: self-giving is the price of Life—of eternal life, of course, for it was Christ who first gave His life, and if we want eternal life we must give ourselves to Him completely. But if we would help another toward finding real Life, we must lay down our lives. If we ourselves want to *live*, let us "lose" it all—and then, miraculously, *find*.

Help me, Lord, to bring this principle down to where I live today. Is there some fear of loss? Some unwillingness to relinquish? Some determination to have it my way? Some insistence on what I "deserve"? May I, by Your strength, let it go, and thus find a greater freedom and a more fulfilling life.

We Have Bargained for a Cross

Before we were married, Jim Elliot wrote exhorting me to lay aside all anxieties and to remember that I had "bargained with Him who bore a *cross.*" It was a word I needed then. It is a word I need now—more than forty years later. Every day there are distractions which easily make me forget that "bargain." If things upset, irritate, or even momentarily bother me, let me think of what Christ endured for me and the contrast will put my troubles in perspective. If I wonder why God deals with me as He does (repeating many times the lessons of love, self-abandonment, acceptance of loss or uncertainty, for example) the only answer I need is that I accepted His invitation to take up my *cross* and follow.

Where Faith Falls Short

The man whose son was demon-possessed (see Mark 9) believed there was some possibility that Jesus could help him, or he would not have bothered to come. Possible? said Jesus. Of course it's possible! "Everything is possible to one who has faith" (Mark 9:23). How much faith would it take to heal this young man? "Probably more than I've got," the father thought. When a man begins to try to *measure* his faith (what "quantity"? What "quality"? Will this do?) he will always find that he comes up short. What to do next? "Help me where faith falls short," (v. 24) is his request. Such a prayer sees oneself as deficient and in need of help. It sees Jesus as able to make up for deficiencies of any kind, even of that which seems most necessary for healing. Will He refuse on the ground that this man ought to manage a more robust belief? Will the father's self-acknowledged failure deprive the son of healing?

Jesus took over. "I command you to come out of him and never go back!" (v. 25). What the father could not do (nor could the disciples) Jesus did. He always responds to faith in Him. We may come without fear, even though we know our faith leaves much to be desired. We may always *come*. He will not turn us away. He will meet us where we are and He will help us where faith falls short.

Wet Shoes and Cold Feet

People are always asking "Do you feel comfortable with this?" (with a position, an idea, even a doctrine or a command) as though a disciple's primary concern were comfort! When the Word is very plain and very hard, we hope for another "interpretation," one we can "relate to," or "feel comfortable" with.

Think of the Son of Man. How much of His earthly life was lived in ease or luxury? He came to obey. He came to die. He came to pay the full price of sin—*my* sin, *your* sin. Do we want to follow Him? Follow *Him*? *His* road?

Samuel Rutherford wrote, "Our soft nature would be borne through the troubles of this miserable life in Christ's arms. And it is His wisdom, who knoweth our mold, that His bairns go wet-shod and cold-footed to heaven." (From *The Loveliness of Christ* [London: Bagster], 23.)

Go Quietly on Your Way

W hen Hananiah prophesied to the captives of the king of Babylon that they would be freed in two years, he told them what they wanted to hear. Jeremiah had just warned them not to pay attention to any prophet who told them not to submit to the king, or that the Lord would soon liberate them. Such prophecies would be false. The Lord was not sending such a prophet. Yet when Hananiah so blatantly disobeyed the Lord and lied to the people, breaking the yoke which God had commanded Jeremiah to wear as a symbol, we find this quiet word: "And the prophet Jeremiah went his way" (Jer. 28:12). So secure was his trust in the God who had sent him, the God in whose strong hands lay the destiny of Israel, that he did not need to take things into his own hands. "The servant of the Lord must not strive" (2 Tim. 2:24, KJV). Jeremiah had done his job faithfully. Opposition, unpopularity, events that seemed disastrous, did not alter his performance of duty or fill him with fear.

Lord, may I today go quietly about the work You have set

me to do, trusting Your absolute control of my life, unafraid of what happens today or what may happen tomorrow. I worship You, my Lord and my King. You are my strength.

Nothing but Crosses?

A t a women's retreat someone asked me if the Christian's life must be all crosses and suffering. "Is there no *happiness* for a believer?" My message that day had been on the great principle of the Cross: *My life for yours*, and I had tried to show how, though we must die many deaths if we truly follow Christ, life will always come from those deaths. The sacrifice will always lead to the song, the laying down of life always to a resurrection. It is the enemy who would have us think always of death—any kind of death—as a dead end. Christ showed us that it is *always*, for the Christian, the gateway to life.

Nothing but crosses? No happiness?

"Thy will but holds me to my life's fruition" (George MacDonald, *Diary of An Old Soul*, April 25). In the path of obedience we shall find the only pure joy to be found anywhere in earth or heaven.

"Goodness and love unfailing, these will follow me all the days of my life" (Ps. 23:6).

No Death Wish

The willingness to be "crucified with Christ" is nothing like the "death wish" that indicates a pathological condition. It is not the desire to be annihilated, but the desire to *live*—to live, that is, as Christ lives. Far from a wish to escape *from* life, it is in fact the wish to escape *into* life, from the chained self. It is Christ I want, Christ who fills my life with His glorious vitality, Christ *living in me,* Christ before me, behind me, beside me. The strongest willing of which my will is capable is to align myself with God, as Christ, in agony in the Garden of Gethsemane, finally aligned Himself with His Father. In doing so—in willing His Father's will—Jesus saved the world. That victory, the "Not I but Christ," conquers the self and conquers the world.

I do not often feel anything like a conqueror. I am a woman, full of womanly fears and concerns and hopes. But my Fortress is a mighty one, a Helper who prevails, "Amid the flood of mortal ills." I trust *Him,* not myself. I live in *Him,* not in myself. In *His* name, not mine, I conquer.

When the Heat Comes

Blessed is the man who trusts in the Lord, and rests his confidence upon him. He shall be like a tree planted by the waterside, that stretches its roots along the stream. When the heat comes it has nothing to fear" (Jer. 17:7-8).

Here is another beautiful metaphor from the created world, illuminating a spiritual principle which is as sure and practical as the natural fact of a tree's need for water. My spirit comes to rest nowhere in all the universe but in the Lord. *There* and nowhere else I find what slakes my thirst, sustains me, causes fruit to appear, and preserves me from fear. I must be *planted*—that is, permanently settled, fixed, and as peaceful as a tree about its assigned place—not in any special "work" or geographical location, necessarily, but in the Lord Himself. Daily I stretch my roots along that fresh, pure stream of His love. I drink living water when I come to Him. Then, when the heat comes, as it is sure to do, I have nothing to fear.

Plant me, Lord. Remind me to stretch my roots to drink of the Water of Life. Refresh me today in Your love, so that in Your coolness I may stand the heat.

The Same Old Routine

It is sometimes supposed that the Holy Spirit is stifled by order, planning, or routine, and can work only in the context of spontaneity, and the "unstructured."

The story of the birth of John the Baptist is an important one in the New Testament. It is worth noting that God's preparations for this event embraced a strictly ordered set of religious routines. The priest Zechariah, to whom this unusual child was to be given, was doing what the rules prescribed. It was the *turn* of his division to take *part* (a clearly defined part) in divine *service*. There was nothing "unstructured" here. "It fell to his lot by priestly custom to enter the sanctuary of the Lord and offer the incense" (Luke 1:9).

It is not unlikely that Zechariah, like the rest of us, sometimes felt wearied by the sameness of his duties and wondered if the ritual was not perhaps empty and meaningless. Was it really worthwhile to go through the routine in the same way, day after day? But this time an angel was waiting for him at the altar! Suppose he had not shown up for his part?

So the Lord meets us—not by our going out of our way and neglecting the usual responsibilities laid upon us, but in the middle of our most repetitive task. There He is, expecting us to come as faithfully as ever, waiting to give us something.

Make me faithful, Lord. Make me humble enough to keep on doing what I know I'm supposed to be doing, and joyfully expectant of finding You close by while I work.

A Powerful Advocate

Their captors hold them firmly and refuse to release them. But they have a powerful advocate, whose name is the Lord of Hosts" (Jer. 50:33-34).

Not many who read this are literal captives of their enemies as Israel and Judah were, but it is possible to be limited and constrained by others in such a way that we feel captive. The One who left heaven for us was put into the hands of sinful men, bound, beaten, and led away to be fastened on a cross. He is our companion and fellow sufferer, understanding well the sense of helplessness that the captive feels.

"Since he himself has passed through the test of suffering, he is able to help those who are meeting their test now" (Heb. 2:18).

Not only does Christ fully understand our test—He can do something about it. He is no longer held by nails on a cross, but stands as our powerful Advocate before God, victor over whatever enemy we face today. The "captivity" may last a while—His did, too—but He can make it shine for you. Bear it in His name and be glad. It will be transformed into a privilege as you offer it back to Him.

Prayer Unites the Heart to God

When we come to God as the humble publican, asking His mercy on us because we are sinners, we are agreeing with God's estimate of us and asking for His remedy. Thus at the onset we are at one with God. Julian of Norwich wrote, "Prayer oneth the soul to God. It is a witness that the soul willeth as God willeth."

Learning to pray has been a lifelong course for me, taking me ever deeper into the mind of Christ, where I find how in need of revision are the patterns of my own thinking. Often the things I have been praying about, things I thought needed to be changed, have remained as they were. But my praying about them has drawn me to the Father, who then has another "chance" (if so I may speak) to change me into the image of His Son.

Choose to Be Strong and Resolute

When the Lord commissioned Joshua to take over from Moses the leadership of His people, these were the words of the commission: Be strong, be resolute.

God appealed directly to the man's will. When a man's will lines up with God's, that is faith. Joshua could have chosen to disobey, but the choice was to be strong or to be weak, to be resolute or to vacillate. Obedience would mean, for Joshua and for all Israel, what it always means for any of us: Life. Nothing less than Life. God was not asking an impossible thing. He never does, for what He asks (or what He commands) He will certainly enable us to do. He was not appealing to Joshua's temperament or moods or natural inclinations, but to his will. Would he obey? Would he accept the charge to be strong and resolute? He would and he did.

The task God has for us today is not the leadership of a great tribe, but, whatever it is, we must choose to be strong—in *His* strength—and to be resolute—by *His* grace. When we bring our wills wholly under that divine strength and that amazing grace, who can estimate the possibilities of such a union?

Vague Prayers

It is a good thing to be specific in prayer. For one thing, it requires thought. What we pray about we should think about. For another, it links the temporal to the eternal—the long list of seemingly impossible tasks to be done or people to be helped is brought before the God of all the Universe. In His presence the needs are seen in a different light. For yet a third reason, we are more apt to expect answers when we ask for definite things.

Often, however, we simply do not know what to ask. Someone's name is brought to the memory with great insistence, a situation looks hopeless and we cannot imagine what even God could do about it—at such times it is a great comfort to know that even the unspecific (even the vague) prayers of an attentive heart are accepted. And the Holy Spirit "within us is actually praying for us in those agonizing longings which never find words" (Rom. 8:26, PHILLIPS).

Be Resolute

A nother minister of the gospel has left his wife. He seems to have followed a familiar pattern: dedication to God, call to the ministry, difficulties, discouragement, loss of self-confidence which turns to loss of confidence in God, resentment, rebellion, and finally the deliberate choice to "worship other gods."

"Be resolute!" said Joshua just before he died at 110. *"You must hold* fast to the Lord ... *Be on your guard* then, love the Lord ... worship Him in loyalty and truth ... *choose* here and now whom you will worship" (Josh. 23:6, 8, 11; 24:14-15).

Responsibility is laid upon us to exercise the wills God gave us. We cannot let go of our wills and wait passively for God or fate or somebody else to do for us what the will was given us to do. We *have* choices. We must resolve. We must purpose to obey. There are powerful forces against which we must be on guard. The only defense is the Lord Himself, who is a mighty Fortress, indeed, our Refuge, our Shield against the enemy. *Run* to Him! *Trust* Him!

A heart turned to Him will be filled with Him.

Help me, Lord, to resist with all my strength the very first beginnings of evil. Grant me *Your* strength and grace.

Your Plans, Lord, Not Mine

L ord, I had planned the day conscientiously—prayer time, breakfast, correspondence that must be mailed today (You know the urgency of the requests I must answer), lunch with a woman whose fellowship I treasure, a speaking engagement tonight which means travel, dinner out with a friend. Then phone calls came, one of them from a woman who wants to stop by "just for a minute or two." What will be left of the afternoon in which I had planned to finish an article, due in five days?

Thank You, Lord, for Psalm 119—

"I tell thee all I have done and Thou dost answer me; teach me thy statutes (v. 26).

"Renew my strength in accordance with thy word (v. 28).

"Keep falsehood far from me and grant me the grace of living by thy law (v. 29).

Troubles That Never Happen

I think Mark Twain said something about having had a lot of troubles in his life, "but most of them never happened." It is legitimate to *plan* for tomorrow but it is not legitimate to *worry* about tomorrow, even when the plan goes awry. Take the interruption as an act of God (no matter how unlike Him it may look!)—or at least as an act He allowed, something wholly under His jurisdiction. Confidently expect Him to fit things together in spite of it. He has promised to do that (see Rom. 8:28). Gracious Father, enable me to depend on You to do what I cannot do. Help me to remember that You depend on me to do what I *can* do.

Worry Is Meddling

Some of us seem to be "by nature" worriers. I know—I am one of them. But this does not in the least excuse me. Worry is forbidden by our Lord as useless. We can't increase our height by worrying, Jesus said. The future is God's business. We are not to meddle with it. We may quietly talk to the Manager if we think trouble is brewing. *He* knows what to do, while we would only create confusion. It is quite impossible simultaneously to believe God *and* to worry. Lord, you are the Blessed Controller of all things. Help me to give up meddling and to leave the matter to You who not only perfectly understand the need but are perfectly able to handle it.

Not by Mere Strength

The songs of both Hannah and Mary for the blessing of motherhood celebrate the sovereignty of a God who can put down the proud and raise the humble. Both recognize that it was not natural gifts or social position or worldly advantages that gained them such blessing and happiness, but the High God Himself, who, as Hannah said, "thunders out of heaven" (1 Sam. 2:10).

It was an unexpected lesson given me from this passage this morning. I was fretting about a disagreement with someone yesterday because, in the light of a new day, I still felt that "my way was best." The Lord seemed to be saying "So what? Granted, of two ways of doing a thing, yours is the more efficient. I am not nearly so concerned with efficiency as I am with your conformity to My Son. Holiness requires that you lay down your 'excellence' sometimes and learn what Hannah learned: not by mere strength shall a man prevail. You must be *put down,* silenced, immobilized—but only in order to see how *I* can work. I will guard the footsteps of my saints (see 1 Sam. 2:9). Trust Me!"

Even in Temptation

It is easy to feel that God has left us alone or turned His attention elsewhere when we are being tempted. The reality of the enemy's presence can dim the sense of God's. But Scripture tells us that Jesus was "led by the Spirit up and down the wilderness and tempted by the devil" (Luke 4:2). I imagine the presence of Satan seemed at times nearly overpowering to Jesus (remember, He was a man, tempted exactly as we are tempted), and He summoned against him the Sword of the Spirit: "It is written." The Spirit had not left Him for a moment, even though the enemy was terribly present, and when the wilderness experience was over, we are told, "Jesus, armed with the power of the Spirit, returned to Galilee" (Luke 4:14).

I do most desperately need that assurance today—the assurance that no matter how powerful the temptation of the enemy may be, and no matter how watery-weak I know myself to be (e.g., I can't concentrate in prayer, or I react with sudden anger to something somebody does), the Holy Spirit has not left me alone. He is here to guide me through my "wilderness," and to *arm* me, as He armed Jesus, with His power.

Having Done All, Stand

There are times when we want desperately to tear into a situation and *do* something. We wish God would do something, and when He seems to be paying no attention to the mess that we are worried about, we are tempted to take things into our own hands. "Stand still" is what He says to us. This morning He reminded me of David's word to Goliath, "The battle is the Lord's" (1 Sam. 17:47). We are to be ready to do anything the Lord our God directs, but if direction is not given, or if we have done all He has said and still the battle is unresolved, then we are simply to *stand*. Standing our ground in prayer means standing by faith against "cosmic powers, against the authorities and potentates of this dark world, against the superhuman forces of evil in the heavens" (Eph. 6:12). It means standing strong with Christ for His victory.

Mighty Captain, show us our part today in Your battle. Make us strong to stand.

Jealousy

The story of Saul and David shows clearly how jealousy leads to fear and fear turns to hatred, hatred to murder. The human heart unless redeemed cannot tolerate a rival. Pride, of course, is at the back of this: *I* am the one who deserves recognition, not he or she. *I* excelled. *I* ought to be the one loved. That honor properly belonged to me, not to him or her. Fear arises as we see our own position threatened, our expectations diverged, our weaknesses, which we thought we had concealed, revealed by the other's success or superiority.

If we take *God* as our refuge, instead of our own ambition or reputation or self-image, and in humility receive whatever He gives us and thank Him for what He gives others, we will be protected from jealousy, that deadly sin which leads so directly to murder in the heart.

Find Joy

When Paul was in prison he wrote a very happy letter to the Christians in Philippi. He used the word *joy* over and over. How did he manage to find joy in such a dark place? Was he some sort of plaster saint, immune to human misery? He was not. He found joy, I believe, because he was always looking for it. Many people are always looking for misery, and it is not hard to find. When they've found it, they tell everybody about it—much more about it than anybody wants to know. Others are continually looking for joy. This is not the same thing as pursuing *happiness*, which depends on *happenings*. Joy depends on Christ living in us, and being allowed to make us joyful. This can happen in the worst of earthly circumstances. From prison Paul wrote, "I wish you joy in the Lord! I will say it again: all joy be yours" (Phil. 4:4). Look for joy in God and you'll find it.

Your Life—His Own Treasure

W hen Abigail, a beautiful and intelligent woman who later became David's wife, saved him from giving way to his anger, she reminded him that because David had fought the Lord's wars, "the Lord your God will wrap your life up and put it with his own treasure" (1 Sam. 25:29). Many instances in the David story show God doing this.

Can we expect the same kind of protection? I believe so—if we are fighting the Lord's wars, standing with Him against unrighteousness of any kind (and that means utmost vigilance against its entering our own camp, our own *hearts*—God give us pure hearts). We must not be afraid. The Lord is not only our shield, He will wrap us up and put us with His own treasure which He knows well how to guard.

The Cross—Day After Day

L ord, could you possibly let me off the hook for a week-
end or so?" is what an energetic old woman I knew
sometimes felt like saying to her Master. I, too, get tired of
obeying. He asks me then, "Do you *want* to be My disciple?"

"Yes, Lord, You know all things—You know I want to."

"The conditions have not changed. Leave self behind. Day
after day take up your cross." (See Luke 9:23.)

"Does this mean the same rigorous routine every day of my
life?"

"It means the cross *I* give you. It means unhesitating obedience to whatever *I* ask on any given day, at any moment.
Remember that, for the disciples, following Me meant coming
apart from the 'routines' at times to rest and pray, and learn of
Me. Trust Me to provide respite when respite is needed."

An Infinite Majesty in the Hands of Men

W hen Jesus had driven an unclean spirit out of a boy, the
onlookers were all "struck with awe at the majesty of
God" (Luke 9:43). While they were still marveling, Jesus had
a private word for the disciples: "'What I now say is for you:
ponder my words. The Son of Man is to be given up into the
power of men.' But they did not understand" (Luke 9:44-45).

The *Te Deum* calls Christ an Infinite Majesty. No wonder

the disciples could not imagine Him whose power over wind, waves, demons, and men they had so often witnessed—*Him,* in the power of men's hands? What could He mean?

But this is the mystery of the gospel. He who spoke and creation sprang at once into being, is the Word made flesh in order to be capable of suffering and death. "For *us* men, and for *our* salvation," says the Nicene Creed.

O Infinite Majesty, once given into men's hands—for *me*— I worship and adore Thee.

Prayer Is a Signature

The question is often raised as to why men should pray when, in the first place, God has already decided what He is going to do, and, in the second place, He already knows everything we might ask. Both questions ignore that we are simply *told* to pray. Prayer, however, is far more than asking for things. When the prophet Nathan told David that he was not the one to build a house for God, David prayed, affirming all that God had done for him and for his people Israel. He declared his faith in God's promises, sure that those promises would come true as always, yet asking God to fulfill His word: "Be pleased now to bless thy servant's house" (2 Sam. 7:29). This was exactly what the Lord had sworn to do. David was signing his name to God's contract, as it were. "This is what I intend to do," God said. "Do it!" said David, and added his signature.

My morning "signature" might be in the words of the

hymn:

> I take Thy promise, Lord, in all its length
> And breadth and fullness as my daily strength,
> Into life's future fearless I may gaze,
> For, Jesus, Thou art with me all the days.
>
> H.L.R. Deck

Israel, Poor Louse!

D^o you ever feel like a poor louse? *Lousy* is the word. We do feel that way when we've sinned against someone, or made a mistake that has caused much trouble for others, or done something that was intended for good but resulted in harm. The enemy, who is always on the lookout for weak spots in our walk, moves in with accusations—"You good-for-nothing! You crumb! You worm! You louse!" and our peace evaporates and we are distracted with remorse, confusion, and "if-onlys."

Then the word of the Lord comes (if we will only shut our ears to the Accuser and open them to our Lord and Redeemer).

"All who take up arms against you shall be as nothing, nothing at all. For I, the Lord your God take you by the right hand; I say to you, Do not fear; it is I who help you, fear not, Jacob you worm and Israel poor louse. It is I who help you, says the Lord, your ransomer, the Holy One of Israel" (Isa. 41:12-14).

God's Delays

I suppose no one, however long he has lived a life of prayer, is immune to the enemy's attack on his confidence that prayer "works." Again and again we are tempted to feel that God is not paying attention, our prayers are futile, why should we keep on praying? Jesus told a story about a widow who made such a nuisance of herself that even a judge who cared nothing for her or for God was finally moved to action. He used this to teach us never to lose heart. "Will not God vindicate His chosen, who cry out to Him day and night, while He listens patiently to them?" (Luke 18:7). A note says that that last phrase may also be translated "While He *delays* to help them." It is worth remembering, when the delays tempt us to quit praying, that He *is* listening patiently—paying attention when we feel He has forgotten all about our prayer, biding *His* time. And He Himself is the very One, remember, who commanded us *to keep on praying and never lose heart*. He *is* listening. He will act. Do not doubt His promise.

He Stood His Ground

Two of the men called "David's heroes," Eleazar and Shammah, are remembered because they *stood their ground*. Eleazar was with David at Pas-Dammim in battle with the Philistines. "When the Israelites fell back, he stood his ground and rained blows on the Philistines until, from sheer weariness, his hand stuck fast to his sword" (2 Sam. 23:10).

Shammah, in a battle which took place in a lentil field, also "stood his ground, saved it, and defeated the Philistines." The significant thing is that in each case the story says, "*So the Lord* brought about a great victory." Another case of how God and man cooperate—the man doing what he could do, and God therefore doing what the man could not do.

So it is when we pray. We have taken ground for God, and there we stand—sometimes so tired of praying for something that it becomes almost automatic—the hand sticks to the sword—and yet we stand. We will see the Lord arise in response to our prayer. He will give victory *because* we have done the only thing we could do—held the ground for Him in prayer.

The Christian's Stand

W hen Jesus predicted the great troubles that would come (destruction of the temple, wars, earthquakes, famines, plagues, terrors, etc.) He promised His followers opportunity to testify and the privilege (the *privilege!*) of being hated for their allegiance to Him. Then He gave them instructions as to what Christians are to do in such times. It is a good word for us in any sort of trouble: Stand firm (see Luke 21:19). This means you must have a solid footing, a dependable place to take your stand. What better than that Firm Foundation, "laid for your faith in His excellent Word"?

Then He describes the terrors in greater detail. When other men are helpless, baffled, fainting, Christians are to hold their heads high, and stand upright (v. 28), knowing that liberation is imminent because God made a promise.

Then Jesus told them to be alert and prayerful, so that they might have strength to pass through all these troubles, and stand in the presence of the Son of Man (v. 36).

Next time we find ourselves even in small troubles, wouldn't it help if, instead of panic, emotional explosion, or complaint, we would simply *stand*—plant our feet on the promises of God, hold our heads up and stand tall, *in the presence,* not merely of the undesired happening, but of the Son of Man Himself who has been through it all?

A Heart With Skill to Listen

S olomon recognized that he could not fulfill his responsibility as king without the help of the Lord. The assignment came from God ("Thou hast made thy servant king"; 1 Kings 3:7) so the qualifications must also come from Him. "I am a mere child, unskilled in leadership," Solomon said, but he did not go on to say, "Therefore make me a great leader." He prayed rather for *a heart with skill to listen* (v. 9).

What a temptation it is, when one is in a position of leadership so that others want to (or must) hear what one has to say—what a temptation to *talk!* The skill of listening must begin with the *heart,* silent and open first to God for *His* word, then ready to hear others before speaking. Solomon listened to

God. He stood—in silence, I should think—before the Ark of the Covenant, the place of the Mercy Seat, before he met the people.

God give me a heart with skill to listen. May I have grace to stand silent before You when I am tempted to open my mouth at once. Help me to cultivate in quietness that skilled heart.

What Will Happen?

W hen some path of obedience lies open to us through a command of the Lord, our first response is often "What will happen to me if I do this?" Grim probabilities take shape in our minds and we set about at once collecting all the reasons why this Scripture cannot apply to us, or why it is quite impossible for *us*, in *our* circumstances, to take this path.

The same response was Obadiah's, comptroller of King Ahab's household, when Elijah appeared and said "Go and tell the king I'm here."

"What will happen?" (1 Kings 18:12), Obadiah replied. "He will kill me." He envisioned Elijah's being mysteriously raptured away, making Obadiah look like a liar. No. It was not possible to obey. Surely Elijah could see the logic of that objection. But the prophet gave the word, and Obadiah, being a "devout worshipper of the Lord" (1 Kings 18:4) obeyed.

Let's quit objecting when a command is given. Try trusting instead, and *see* what will happen. He has power to prevent what you imagine will happen, and power to do what you cannot begin to imagine. "And Ahab went to meet Elijah" (v. 16).

Permanent Fence-Sitters

E lijah challenged the people to get off the fence. If the Lord was God, serve Him. If not, serve the others. We are given opportunity daily to reopen the question—Is God really God? Yes—when He does what I think He ought to. No—when He doesn't. I'll trust Him while things are going my way, I'll reopen the question when things fall apart. Sovereign? Well—I think so. Loving? Some of the time. Able to save to the uttermost? Hmmm.

He *is* God. Settle it. Be still and know it. Refuse to consider. The decision is a lifetime decision, and when "other gods" ring the doorbell, we need not bother to answer, except to remind ourselves, "The King of Glory is the Lord of Hosts," Him alone I will trust and obey.

Frame Your Heart to the Burden

M any things laid on us by life, by circumstances—let's face it—*by the Lord Himself,* are not at all to our liking. We complain that they do not fit. They weigh us down, hem us in, frustrate, annoy, destroy. They are the cause of wipeout, freak-out, burnout, dropout.

But those are excuses. The truth is we do not want them. They were not in *our* plan. It is resentment of the burdens, not the burdens themselves, that destroys us. It is the unwillingness to shoulder them in company with Christ.

But there is another way.

Samuel Rutherford wrote, "How sweet a thing were it for us to make our burdens light by framing our hearts to the burden and making our Lord's will a law." Get under the load gladly. "This needs to be carried by someone—*I'll* carry it, Lord, with *You*." That attitude—that "frame of heart," we could call it, will radically change both us *and* the burden. We'll be amazed at its featherweight.

"Take my yoke," said Jesus. "My yoke *is* easy, and my burden is light" (Matt. 11:29-30, KJV).

Sit Quietly

Of the two sisters whom Jesus visited often, it seems that Martha was the take-charge one. Perhaps she was the older. She was the one who made Jesus welcome (Luke 10:38) and felt responsible for the meal, while Mary sat herself down to listen to Jesus. Martha fretted and fussed. This called forth a rebuke from Jesus. Nobody needs to fret and fuss about anything.

The Israelites were rebuked for "turmoil and tumult and all their restless ways" (Ezek. 7:11). It had caused all sorts of abominations—insolence, injustice, violence.

Pascal once observed that most of man's troubles resulted from his inability to sit quietly in his room. It is worth thinking about. Today's turmoil and trouble may be seen in God's perspective if we will take time, go into a room and shut the door, sit down, and be quiet before Him. He is *God*. He is in charge. Be still and know that.

Choose the Better

Mary and Martha had made choices. It seems that Martha may have chosen a menu that was too elaborate. A simple one would have sufficed, and left her time to sit down with Jesus and Mary. Mary's choice was better.

Sometimes our difficulty arises from unreasonable expectations—of ourselves, of what we can accomplish in a given time, or of others, of their abilities or temperaments. We stew over failure (again—ours or others') instead of quietly giving it over to Christ, thanking Him for *His* strength in place of our weakness, and then simply going on in peace.

"O Lord, make us, we implore Thee, so to love Thee that Thou mayest be to us a Fire of Love purifying and not destroying" (Christina Rossetti).

A Continual Transformation

What is it that makes a Christian "shine"? Paul explains it in his second letter to the Corinthians. As we look steadily to the Lord, "beholding" or "reflecting" His glory, we are being changed into His likeness from one degree of glory to another (see 2 Cor. 3:18). The Greek verb is present tense, showing action going on now—that is, effective as long as we keep our eyes on the Lord and not on ourselves or anybody else. W.J. Conybeare's translation is "The glory which shines upon us is reflected by us." The moon shines steadily with the sun's glory so long as earth doesn't get in the way.

Shine on me, Lord of Light, and let no shadow of anything temporal (possessions, people, ambitions, fears, anger, despair, or anything whatsoever) come between us.

Why Doesn't He Intervene?

L azarus was sick. His sisters sent word to Jesus, sure that He would come immediately to heal him. But Jesus did not budge. So it happens sometimes with us. We are in urgent need of God's help. We ask for it. It does not come. We easily conclude that God is not listening, or that He does not care about our concerns, or that all the promises of His love have broken down.

Read the story in John 11: "Though he loved Martha and her sister and Lazarus, after hearing of his illness Jesus waited for two days" (v.6). Loving and waiting. The two things do not seem to us to go together, not in the middle of our particular situation. But the story lights up a facet we would miss: the glory of God is wrought *through* suffering and death which are strictly temporary. God is engineering things we can hardly dream of. Lazarus' story opens our eyes. He was indeed very ill. Mary and Martha were desperate. He died. *Then* Jesus came. Lazarus' resurrection, revealing the authority of God over the worst powers at work in our world, shows us His glory.

Can we pray for literal resurrection like Lazarus'? *In God's time* He will do it. Some day His glory will be revealed because of this thing we are desperate about. Remember it is because He loves us that He waits. Immediate intervention would abort the far greater thing He has in mind. Trust Him for the greater.

Radiant With Hope

M ay the God of hope fill *you* with joy and peace in your faith, that by the power of the Holy Spirit, your whole life and outlook may be radiant with hope" (Rom. 15:13, PHILLIPS).

This was Paul's prayer for the Romans, a group of Christians he had not yet met, but he knew they were a mixed bag—Jews and non-Jews—and were tempted to look down on one another. It was always the prayer of my dear spiritual mother for me. She knew my nature—not a hopeful one. Faith raises the Christian's sights from the conflicts and discouragements that are our routine experience in a broken world to Him who holds out the very real hope of triumph. It is not a forlorn hope. It is assured, for by His Cross and passion Christ has overcome the world. This confidence is enough reason for joy and peace. It is *enough,* if I dwell on it by faith, and by the Spirit's power, to make even my whole life and outlook radiant with hope.

The Secret of Understanding

The man who has received my commands and obeys them—he it is who loves me; and he who loves me will be loved by my Father; and I will love him and will disclose myself to him" (John 14:21).

Have you felt that you were stumbling along more or less in the dark, wishing now and then for a more vital spirituality, a greater understanding of God, and more "love" for Him? Obedience is the secret of spiritual insight. It is not given to any but those who obey, for they are the *only* ones who love God. There is no love where there is no obedience. To choose to disobey is to choose darkness. No wonder we stumble. Open your heart to the Light by doing what God says. Then He will know you as His true lover, will love you and disclose Himself to you. And you will walk in the light.

Something Much Smaller

Has it ever happened with you that you have asked God to show you what He wants done about a certain matter, and His answer seems to be, "I am concerned now with something much smaller"? He sometimes shows me that the thing that looms large in importance to me is not nearly so important to God just now. He would rather I please Him in some "minor" thing. This is the thing that matters at the moment.

A husband or wife may be thinking of some special occasion when he or she can demonstrate love, but what the other longs for is something much smaller—some word or touch or look of real tenderness. The big occasion, the expensive gift, may appear empty of meaning unless the love is evident in little ways day by day.

The life of Christ, if it is to be lived daily, is lived out in love. This love will be manifest in our desire to offer up every *least* thing to Him, to do the smallest task faithfully, confess the "little" sins quickly, be strict with our minutes as well as our hours.

"Do you love me?" Jesus asks.

"Why, of course, Lord—look what I did for you last Sunday at church!"

"But child—I am looking for something much smaller."

Visible Threats, Invisible Protection

Three times in as many weeks a family I know has experienced near-disaster. They were protected each time by what seemed a very narrow margin.

When the king of Aram sent horses and chariots to capture the prophet Elisha, because Elisha seemed to be able to read his very thoughts, the prophet's disciple was terrified. "Oh, master," he said, "which way are we to turn?" In answer to Elisha's prayer, his eyes were opened—that is, to him was given faith to see what had been invisible—and he realized that the hills were covered with horses and chariots of fire. The forces sent to protect them were far more powerful than the strong forces of the king (see 2 Kings 6).

Whatever may be the threat we face, we can rest in the confidence that we are surrounded by heavenly protection capable of demolishing every lesser force. Nothing can possibly touch us without our Captain's permission. He gives permission. He will personally accompany us into the fire or through the deep water. There is no need to be afraid.

"I Cannot Act by Myself"

These are startling words, coming from the lips of Jesus (John 5:30). We tend to think of Him as all-powerful, yet here He is, telling us He is all-helpless. His authority and power were not His own, but given by His Father. His aim was not His own will (see John 5:30) but the will of Him who sent Him. It is a piece of huge arrogance in us to think we can manage by ourselves. We'll manage, all right, but all we shall ever succeed in doing by ourselves is making a mess of our lives. If our aim is the same as our Master's, to do the will of the Father, *we cannot act by ourselves.* This means we must be consistently *asking* for help and *accepting* whatever help God sends.

"Lord, this is not quite what I meant," is sometimes our response to His answer.

"What is your aim?" He asks us then, "Your will or Mine?"

"Yours, Lord."

"Then remember: you cannot act by yourself."

No Home, No Love, No Welcome

It is a chilling series Jesus cites to describe the attitude of the Jews who were determined to kill him (see John 5:38, 42-43). There was in their hearts no *home* for the Word. They pored over it, but refused to come to the very One of whom it spoke. There was no *love* for God in them—they were far more concerned with men's opinions. And there was, naturally, no *welcome* for Christ Himself. How could there be if they received neither the testimony of the Word nor the Father's accreditation of Him?

From this stoniness save us, Lord. You cannot be at home

where our own honor matters more than Yours, or where the knowledge of Scripture takes the place of the real Life of Christ living in us. Help us, O God, not only to study Your Word, but to trust and obey it, that Christ may find in us a home, an honest love, and a warm welcome.

"But I Don't Feel *Very Loving"*

Most of us "feel" very little love for people we don't know, and, if we are honest, we'll admit we don't even feel much for many of the people we do know. How in the world are we supposed to drum up the proper feelings?

Peter tells us in his first letter (1 Pet 1:22) you can't start with the feelings themselves. They won't be corralled. You have to begin by *obedience to the truth.* This, in turn, *purifies the soul.* When the muck and sediment are filtered out, you will "feel sincere affection towards your brother Christians." You will be enabled then to "love one another whole-heartedly with all your strength."

We may pray, "O Lord, help me to love So-and-So," but God may be saying, "*You* do what *you* can first—obey the truth and so purify your soul. Only then can I give you love."

Divine Healing and Miracles

It has sometimes been a matter of heated debate among Christians whether to use medicine or to expect "divine" healing.

All healing, of course, is "divine," in that it could not happen if God did not give it. But God nearly always, both in biblical times and today, uses some human instrumentality to accomplish His work. When the prophet Isaiah had told Hezekiah he would die, Hezekiah prayed and God gave him fifteen "extra" years. This answer came through the prophet, who then told the king's servants to apply a fig plaster. They did so, and the boil healed (see 2 Kings 20:1-7).

Let us not be so arrogant as to demand from God "special" signs and miracles. Let us humbly pray, and then both trust Him for *His* answer in *His* way and time, and obey whatever simple little thing He may ask us to do toward that end. The fig plaster does not take the place of the divine touch.

Divine Healing and God's Glory

Could not this man, who opened the blind man's eyes, have done something to keep Lazarus from dying?" (John 11:37).

This was the quite natural question asked by some of the Jews when they saw Jesus weep on His way to the grave of His friend. "He has performed some quite astounding miracles. Here is His friend—surely He could have *done something!*"

Faith knows that with God all things are "possible," in one sense. Of course the prevention of Lazarus' death was within the scope of Jesus' power—*if* such healing could have shown the glory of God. Jesus knew what Lazarus' sisters, Mary and Martha, and their friends, did not know—that in this case the glory of God would be revealed more gloriously than by what they had expected. Jesus could indeed have "done something," but was about to do something else, something that never entered their heads.

"If you have faith you will see the glory of God," He said. Mary and Martha had faith. The corpse answered Jesus' summons and *came out of the tomb* (see John 11:40).

We cannot demand answers in our own terms. We are to trust Him, to whom we bring our prayers, to work in the way which will most perfectly glorify God. We can *count on* that answer, though the delay be much longer than four days.

Might and Joy

D oes it not often happen that at the very time set aside to worship the Lord, a matter of serious concern looms larger in importance than prayer itself?

One morning I was preoccupied by concern for the care and well-being of someone for whom I am responsible. Many uncertainties faced me. This word shone out of my morning's reading, from David's ordained Offering of Thanks. "Might and joy are in his dwelling" (1 Chron. 16:27). His dwelling, His kingdom—the place where His will is done—is where I am to live every day, as an obedient worshipper. Therefore, although my human situation may be one of helplessness and anxiety, I move by faith into that realm of might and joy. They are God's might, God's joy, and He gives them lavishly to any of us who will take them.

What is your weakness or worry today? Leave it to God. Instead, take His might, His joy, and be thankful!

He Will Find a Place

Uncertainty is surely, for most of us, one of the harder lessons in faith. We look ahead and see only darkness, or what may seem more frightening—possibilities we're convinced we can't cope with.

This is where I am this morning as I write—the possibilities of what may happen are daunting. Asking the Lord for some help in resting my case with Him, I found these words: "You saw ... how the Lord your God carried you all the way to this place, as a father carries his son. In spite of this you did not trust the Lord your God, who went ahead on the journey to find a place for your camp" (Deut. 1:31-33).

Has He, in fact, carried me all the way to this place? Of course He has.

Did He look after my needs as attentively as a father his son's?

Of course He did.

Have I reason to doubt that He is even now going ahead of me on my journey, to *find a place* for me?

No reason whatever.

Shall I trust Him then? Lord, forgive my fears. I will trust, and not be afraid. The place You find will certainly be a place of peace.

Plunged Into Grief ... For Your Good

T his is a strange succession of words, isn't it? What sort of person wants to see another plunged into grief? Jesus spoke these words to His disciples about His own departure from them. He understood their human feelings, and mentioned them matter-of-factly. He did nothing to spare their feelings. Nothing could change the fact that His going would cause *grief* to the ones He loved best. Nothing could change the necessity of His going. He *would* leave, and they *would* sorrow. It was inexorable.

So it is very often in this sorrowing, broken world. Certain things must happen and certain people must suffer, and God does not intervene *at the moment* to exempt them from suffering. But He does do something. He is not oblivious up there, doing nothing. He has a plan which is also fitting together. He will give us something better. Unimaginable? Of course, as it was unimaginable for the poor disciples who didn't want the Holy Spirit—they wanted their Master.

Choose for us, God, nor let our weak preferring
Cheat us of good Thou hast for us designed.
Choose for us, God, Thy wisdom is unerring,
And we are fools and blind.

From "Still Will We Trust"

Faith Leads to Certainty

Very few things in this world are certain. We can pretty well count on death and taxes. But the Christian lives in two worlds—a visible one and an invisible one. The latter is the world of reality, permanence, certainty, a world apprehended by that seemingly flimsiest of means, faith. But it is not flimsy. It is not a mere feeling, but an act of will which takes hold of God's faithfulness. In Jesus' prayer of John 17 He tells His Father that the men the Father has given Him *know with certainty* that Jesus came from God, for they *have had faith to believe* that God sent Him. How else could they have known with certainty? Jesus' life on earth—the deeds He did (many of them miraculous) and the words He spoke—did not by any means convince everybody that He had come from God. There was hot contention over who He was and who He said He was. Religious leaders refused to believe, and *therefore did not know.*

The man or woman who wants to know Him must start by believing Him. Today also, even though I have "believed" for many years, I am required to lay hold afresh on His promises to lead and care for me. I am tempted not to believe them, but I will in His name refuse the temptation.

God's Hands or Men's?

Most of us at some time have felt ourselves to be helpless and at the mercy of people who are "out to do us in." We cry "Help!" and help doesn't come. Has God forgotten us? Panic sets in, and we shiver and shake like captive animals. Our faith seems to be of no use anymore because these people have us where they want us and prayer seems a mockery.

Remember when Jesus was a captive, and at the mercy of the Judean procurator, Pilate? Pilate claimed that he had authority to release Jesus or to crucify Him, whichever he happened to choose. Was Jesus intimidated? He knew there was not a single second when He was not being held secure in His Father's hands. "You would have no authority at all over me ... if it had not been granted you from above" (John 19:11).

We are always held by those same strong hands. Never mind, then, *why* power is granted to others to do you wrong—that is God's affair, not yours. Mind only the fact that they couldn't possibly touch you if God didn't permit it, and then *trust* Him. He will see you through.

Make Me a Servant

Last week a lady said to me, "I've never asked God to make me a servant—not in the *physical* sense, anyway. I was afraid He might do it."

A servant does not have a choice as to the kind of work he

will do. He is at his master's service, ready to do as he is told. Do we dare to think of ourselves as God's servants as long as *we* are the ones laying down the terms? "This I'll do, that I won't do." "*Spiritual* work? Yes, Lord. *Physical* work? No, Lord."

Think of Christ. In order to do the Father's will He had to become *physical*. The Eternal Word had to empty Himself and be subjected to all the weaknesses and limitations and humiliations of becoming a baby, a boy, a man, a *crucified* man.

Who do we think we are?

Lord, forgive my arrogance. I surrender the choices to You. Make me a servant—*any* kind of servant, ready to do *any* kind of work so long as it's what You need done.

Don't Let Your Courage Fail

T hese are words we all need to hear from time to time. We need to hear them spoken by somebody else, for they come with more power than when we are only telling ourselves.

God sent a man named Azariah to King Asa of Judah to cheer him on when he might have been tempted to quit struggling against godlessness. Azariah, by the Spirit of God, reminded him of God's presence with him, His willingness to be found by those who look for Him, and His deliverance from enemies in the past. Then he said, "But now you must be strong and not let your courage fail; for your work will be rewarded" (2 Chron 15:7). We do need to be assured that what we are trying to do is worthwhile. If it is for God, an effort to stand against anything that opposes Him and to stand, humbly and even alone if necessary, *for* His kingdom, we can be perfectly sure our work is not useless. It will be rewarded in God's time. Don't let your courage fail!

Strong in Thy strength, safe in Thy keeping tender,
We rest on Thee, and in Thy name we go.

From "We Rest on Thee,"
a hymn by Edith G. Cherry

Not Your Battle

Fear arises when we imagine that everything depends on us. We assume burdens God never meant us to carry. How much better to take whatever is troubling us immediately to God, confess our helplessness and perplexity, and then do the next thing. The story of how Jehoshaphat responded when news came of hordes of enemies about to attack should furnish some clues for us.

"Jehoshaphat, in his alarm, resolved to seek guidance of the Lord" (2 Chron. 20:3). He proclaimed a fast, and in front of the people, prayed. He remembered who God was, His power and help in the past, stated his case regarding the present threat, and acknowledged his own powerlessness. "We know not what we ought to do; we lift our eyes to thee" (2 Chron. 20:12). God answered through a prophet, "Have no fear ... the battle is in God's hands, not yours" (v. 15) What a relief!

But there *were* things for the *people* to do:

Stand firm.

Wait.

Do not fear.

Go out and face the enemy.

Next morning early they set out, and Jehoshaphat told them, "Hold firmly to your faith ... and you will be upheld" (v. 20). Then he appointed men to *sing!* Going to meet the hordes they so desperately feared, they sang.

Make sure you are on God's side, whatever today's "battle" may be. Then do what Jehoshaphat did. Stand firm, wait, don't be afraid, go and face the enemy, sing.

Our Sennacheribs

S ennacherib was the Assyrian king who threatened Judah, believing he could attach them to his own kingdom. Judah's king, Hezekiah, set about blocking up the springs, fortifying the walls, and reminding his people of the source of their trust. It was not military measures that were to give them confidence. Hezekiah encouraged them to be strong and brave because "We have more on our side than he has. He has human strength; but we have the Lord our God to help us and to fight our battles" (2 Chron. 32:7-8).

The foes we face today will be of a different nature— godless legislation, an "impossible" human relationship, the oppression of tremendous sorrow in our own lives or the lives of people we love, the pressures of time and duties which seem beyond our strength—these are our Sennacheribs who taunt us to quit trusting the God of Heaven. "Look what happens to people who put their trust in *Him!*" they say to us. It's a plight to be in, all right, as was Hezekiah's. But Scripture says, "In this plight King Hezekiah and the prophet Isaiah ... cried to heaven in prayer. So the Lord sent an angel" (vv. 20-21).

Take heart today! The Lord our God is still receiving the prayers of those who put their trust in Him instead of in human strength. No Sennacherib on earth or in hell can defeat Him or His faithful ones.

Small Change

We have promised the Lord our loyalty and lifelong obedience, "at any cost." We imagine perhaps having to pay the high price of death itself—losing our loved ones, or losing our own lives in the line of service. We are not prepared for the "low" costs of the spiritual life, the petty sacrifices we must make daily (according to the wish of another in some simple thing, saying no to ourselves about a piece of cake, for example), if we are to follow faithfully. We keep the small change in our pockets, as it were, instead of gladly turning it over to Him who can multiply even a widow's "mite" for blessing. She who gives is blessed as well as—no, even more than—the ones who receive.

Lord, if I overlook the "pennies" You give me to give back to You, You will never be able to ask me to give You the dollars. Make me faithful every hour of every day in that which looks trivial at the moment.

All We Need to Know

John 15:11—"I have spoken ... joy."
John 16:1, 4—"I have told you ... faith."
John 16:33—"I have told you ... peace."
"In the world you will have trouble. But courage! The victory is mine. I have conquered the world" (v. 33).

When we are in the center of trouble, so that it surrounds and seems to close us in, we panic and cry in desperation, "God, get me out of here!" He does not by any means always answer that cry as we hope. Nor does He give us His reasons for not answering, apart from the above. Isn't it reason enough that God's refusals furnish the context in which we may learn joy, faith, peace, and courage? Is that not enough to settle our "why"?

A Salt Land

Being human, we are daily tempted to lean for support on humankind. If we do this *instead* of trusting in the Lord, so that our hearts are weaned away from Him and begin to be fixed on some individual who has proved to be very helpful and loving and sympathetic, we will become like the one described by Jeremiah the prophet: "... A juniper in the desert; when good comes he shall not see it. He shall dwell among the rocks in the wilderness, in a salt land where no man can live" (Jer. 17:6).

It is a subtle thing that can happen. A good friendship goes bad because we become too dependent on one person, forgetting Him who alone can slake our deepest thirst. Gradually we become blind to His goodness. We feel rejected and helpless and begin to feel more and more resentful and self-pitying. The other person feeds these sins, and before we know it we are living in a wilderness of bare rocks, a salt land where no one can live, when all the time fresh springs flow nearby if only we would turn and trust and drink.

Thy Shining-Place

O make my mirror-heart Thy shining-place!" prayed George MacDonald. The prayer fit my special need this morning. A matter arose for prayer, entailing perhaps a decision several months from now, for which, if it does become a necessary decision, I need God's wisdom and heart-preparation. My heart is a mirror, often smudged by the world and by my own selfishness. The reflection of Christ cannot be clear if the mirror is not clean.

Lord, make it clean. Shine there, I pray, that "the light of revelation—the revelation of the glory of God in the face of Jesus Christ" (2 Cor. 4:6) be faithfully reflected.

He Shall Sit As a Refiner

T he refiner of silver, we are told, continues the melting and heating and removing of impurities until he can see his face reflected in it. We are tested and purified in order that the image of Christ may be clear in us.

"Why doesn't God *do* something?" we cry, when the heat is on. He is doing something—something absolutely vital. It may seem that He is passive when we wish He were active, but the truth is that He is *sitting*—not idly, but as a refiner and purifier of silver.

Rich Enough for the Need

C an God possibly do anything about the matter that troubles me most today? Isn't it really a bit much to expect?

In one form or other, articulated or not, this thought does occur to most of us now and again. Think about it: Can He? Does He have what it takes? Well, think about these facts:

He made the stars.

He created the "great lights"—and once made the sun stand still for Joshua.

He combined the elements with perfect precision of atomic and molecular structure—and once caused an iron axehead to float.

He owns the cattle on a thousand hills, as well as New

Zealand's ninety million sheep—but was Himself led as a sheep to the slaughter and became the Lamb which takes away the sin of the world.

Is He able to do what I ask? Is He rich enough for my need? He is. I found the promise this morning in Romans 10:12— "Lord of all ... rich enough for the need of all who invoke him." The context, of course, is salvation. If He can *save* us, He can save us "to the uttermost." Doesn't that cover everything I need?

Rescued Through Suffering
(Job 36:15)

H ere is another of the Lord's many words of comfort to those who suffer. It was spoken by the young man Elihu, the last one to try to "comfort" Job. None of the others had made a dent, and we have no reason to suppose Elihu did either, but he spoke the truth: those who suffer He rescues through suffering, and teaches them by the discipline of affliction.

It is always our salvation that God is working on. While we are actually *on* the ash heap it is next to impossible for anyone to get through to us. We are convinced that *our* situation is unique and *they* have no idea what we suffer. There is One who understands it thoroughly, and He waits to reveal Himself if we will look away from the blinding trouble and look up to Him. The very suffering, this word tells us, is God's means of rescue. Without it, we would have lost sight of things that matter far more than the things we have lost. God is a ploughman, and, as Rutherford said, "He purposeth a crop."

Dwell in Christ, Dwell in Love

I am at sixes and sevens just now—perplexed by many affairs of business and personalities and social obligations. The faith I need is of the sort that holds on to Christ's words, "Dwell in me.... Dwell in my love" (John 15:4, 10). He gave these commands to the despairing disciples before He went to die. "Settle down," He was saying. "Just stay where you are—in *Me*. I am staying with you and in you. Make your home in My love. Rest here. Take My peace." To go on from one day to the next, leaving the unsettling things with God, being free and whole and *serene* because we are secure in our home—this is what "dwelling" in Christ and His love means. The people and the things about which we simply do not know what to do we can commit to His love as well, asking Him to find a room for them.

The Prerequisite for Discernment

It is not reasonable to talk of wanting to know God's will unless we have first offered ourselves to Him. Why should He show us what to do if we have not yet made up our minds as to whose we are? The will of God is for those who trust Him—those, that is, who commit themselves totally, who offer their "very selves to Him as a living sacrifice, dedicated and fit for His acceptance" (Rom. 12:1). This must always be the first step, followed by the refusal to allow the world to dictate thought patterns. The mind must be "remade"—shaped according to a radically different pattern. Then and only then can we discern the will of God. Then we will understand that it is, contrary to the view that comes naturally, "good, acceptable, and perfect."

Unwitting Sins

Is the bleakness of this world of mine a reflection of my poverty or my honesty ... an indication that I have strayed from my path or that I am following it?" (Dag Hammerskjold, *Markings* [London: Faber & Faber], 56).

We cannot by any means always be certain that we are on the "path of righteousness," even though the Lord our Shepherd promises to lead us there. We are wayward and sinful. "Who is aware of his unwitting sins?" wrote the psalmist (see Ps. 19:12). "Cleanse me of any secret fault." Trust means to go on in the path that *seems* right, willing to take the condemnation of others, willing even to face the possibility that their condemnation may prove just in the end. The Lord alone knows the secrets of the heart. We are naked before Him, we can rest in His love, we can trust Him to show us, in His own time, whatever we need to know. We *must* trust Him for that—we certainly cannot trust ourselves or anyone else.

"Let integrity and uprightness protect me, for I have waited for thee, O Lord" (Ps. 25:21).

Defend and Deliver Me, Lord

T his is a prayer to pray when fears overtake us that we shall go astray and be defeated at last. "*Put* your trust in the Lord"—how repeatedly in Scripture this command is given, in one way or another. Expect Him to defend you from fear itself, from an endless raising of "what ifs" and "but, Lords." Let your imagination come to rest in His Word of promise. Don't let it moil in the frightening possibilities—there will be plenty of grace at hand if any of those should come to pass, and that's really all that matters. Go on with the work God has given you. He will "defend and deliver." Go on in peace (see Ps. 25:20).

Incense

"We are indeed the incense offered by Christ to God." *We?* That's what the Book says. We who believe, whose sins are under the blood, we are actually a pure and fragrant offering which the Son presents to His Father. How is it possible? "Who is equal to such a calling?" (2 Cor. 2:15, 17). Not one of us possesses in himself the least qualification. It is Christ who, by offering Himself, qualifies us to become an offering acceptable to God. Then and only then can we present our bodies as a living sacrifice to Him. Then and only then—because Christ has first been offered and has offered us—are we "holy," "acceptable to God."

I write this just after having sinned greatly against someone I love. What I did I had meant for good, but it turned into an offense. I am a sinner, and deeply aware of it this morning—yet, having confessed it, I am, through Christ, fragrant incense. What mercy and what grace!

I Am Your Salvation

When we find ourselves in what we think is an intolerable situation—the kind of which we say, "But this *can't* go on"—it is tempting to pray that God will get us out of it, stop it somehow, change things, make people do (or not do) something. Why doesn't He *answer* us? Is He deaf? Are the heavens brass? Doesn't He care? He hears. Heaven is open. He cares. But He has something much greater in mind. It would be simple enough, I suppose, for Him to do the thing we demand if He didn't really care. But of course this reasoning is silly. He is working out His design for a universe, for an eternity, and His interest lies in drawing our hearts up and out of the prison of self. He says to us, "*I* am your salvation" (Ps. 35:3). He wants us to see *glory*, to breathe *fresh* air, to walk in *light*, to come to *Him* for rest. We can't do that if He is always getting us out of the very situation He has arranged for us to learn in.

Our prayer today:

"Let me hear Thee declare I am thy salvation."

What Else Do You Need?

R eading the psalms is a good way to adjust the focus of our praying. So much that occupies us is petty. This morning I woke thinking of some new clothes I had just bought, not certain they were quite what I had wanted. As I went to prayer I realized how insignificant a matter it was, and the psalm for the day adjusted my focus to the truly (and ultimately) significant:

Thy unfailing love;
Thy faithfulness;
Thy righteousness;
Thy judgments;
Thy wings;

Thy house;
Thy delights;
Thy light (see Ps. 36).

This Moment's Need

T he urgency of some matter at hand—a family member ill
or rebellious or unemployed or estranged, a sudden disaster, an impending disaster, or whatever it may be—sends us
to desperate prayer. Yesterday's list seems too high for us in
such a moment, too rarified. But can we not find in it what we
need, even in this terrible moment? God's absolute depend-
ability—

to care;
to be true to His promise;
to do what is best;
to see the truth of the situation;
to protect;
to provide;
to satisfy;
to guide.

Have we any need that is not covered here? The message is
Trust Me. Whatever the specifics, if we are saying "Yes, Lord,
but," He is saying *Trust Me.* That is every moment's greatest
need.

Two Things You Can Always Do

Is there any restlessness worse than the kind that comes when we feel that *something* must be done but we cannot for the life of us figure out *what*. We are afraid, frustrated, guilty, angry, and helpless all at the same time. Be at peace! There are two definite things you can always do, no matter how bad the situation.

"How deep I am sunk in misery, groaning in my distress:

1. *Yet* I will wait for God;
2. I will praise him continually" (Ps. 42:5, 11).

There they are. Try them. Set your mind on the One who is in charge, trust Him to work things out according to His perfect plan ("God has no problems, only plans!" said Corrie ten Boom). While you are waiting, *sing*.

God's Message or Satan's?

It is not always clear to us, living down here in the murk of a fallen world, whether a thing comes from God or from Satan, whether "God did it" or "the devil did it." Let us be very clear about one thing—God never *does* evil, but any evil that touches us can be turned to His own good purpose. He is sovereign. He's got the whole world in His hands. Nothing can ever happen to separate us from His love.

The "thorn" or "sharp pain" *given* to Paul was a messenger of Satan to bruise him—but he goes right on to show why God permitted it: "to save me from being unduly elated" over a certain thrilling spiritual experience (see 2 Cor. 12:7).

Satan is given leeway in the lives of Christians. Make no mistake about that. But God is always setting limits, always in control, always drawing us toward holiness. Trust Him for that. Believe in the Love that will never let go.

Impossible Situations

Thou hast caught us in a net,
Thou hast bound our bodies fast;
Thou hast let men ride over our heads.
We went through fire and water (Ps. 66:11-12).

We all know the feelings the psalmist described here. Our contexts of experience differ greatly, but the same Lord rules our world now and works through what seems to us insoluble. He is "tremendous in His dealings with mankind," (v. 5), or, as an older translation has it, "terrible in His doings with the children of men." Whether it looks tremendous or terrible to us just now, we can take our peace from the knowledge that it is our God who has "caught us," "bound our bodies," allowed men to "ride over our heads"—because He has a loving purpose. As in ancient myths and fairy tales, the prize is always gained through some fearful ordeal, some dark and dangerous passage, some encounter with fire, water, or dragons.

"But Thou hast brought us out" (He is *bringing* us, every minute. He is not off somewhere else, but beside us, protecting, leading) *"into liberty."* That is what He wants for us: Freedom at last, release from ourselves, entrance into the broad meadows of His love.

"Blessed is God who has not withdrawn His love and care from me" (v. 20).

The Rough Road to Freedom

The lines from yesterday's psalm speak of the helplessness of prey, caught in a net—a sudden inexplicable cessation of normal activity; of being bound fast—immobilized, prevented from escape, deprived of our power to help; of being "ridden over"—crushed, conquered, destroyed, perhaps even cheated out of something which properly belonged to us; and of going through fire and water—both purifiers, both terribly dangerous if not under control. But the wonderful thing in the psalm is the recognition that it is God Himself, the one who gave us life and keeps our feet from stumbling (Ps. 66:9) who is now refining us—using net, cords, ruthless people, fire, and water as His agents to give us freedom. It is a rough road, of course. But nothing worth having comes cheaply. It is through "much tribulation," Jesus told us, that we will enter the kingdom.

Lord, give us courage. Make us faithful. Help us to *praise* You.

Two Sides of a Coin

D oes God choose some to whom He wants to give salvation? Can I do anything at all about it? These are hard questions that touch on deep mysteries ("predestination," "free will," "election," to mention some of the theological labels). We cannot pretend intellectual satisfaction with regard to such questions. We know that love and obedience are far more necessary than understanding of theology. But God has made clear over and over again in the Bible that *He* works and *man* works. That is how He arranged things. That is His design. He searches the hearts of men, always looking for *faith.* Who trusts Him? Who is willing to receive what He wants to give? Who recognizes his own inadequacy? To that one He comes, He gives, He answers.

In a single verse we find much light: "Righteousness ... comes from faith in Christ, given by God in response to faith" (Phil. 3:9). There it is. The righteousness is all His, only His. It can't be bought or earned. It can only be given. It *will* be given—when somebody trusts Him for it. God gives, we receive. Two sides of the coin called salvation.

Strength for Anything

Paul writes to the Christians in Philippi about his prison experience, but without any descriptive detail. He might have dwelt on how dreadful the place was and how uncomfortable to be in stocks or chained to two guards. His letter is filled with *joy*, with loving concern, with gratitude. He cheers those who were probably trying to think of ways to cheer him. He has been "very thoroughly initiated into the human lot with all its ups and downs" (Phil. 4:12), and assures his friends, "I have strength for anything through him who gives me power" (v. 13).

Think of those words! *Strength for anything.* They are for us today. Something, perhaps, looms ominously in our imagination. "I'll never be able to do that," "What will we do if...," "She won't be able to stand it if...," "I can't take it." For any such threat, remember who it was who gave Paul strength. He stood by him in his cell. He stands by you today. He will give you *strength for anything*—if you ask Him for it. Don't be afraid. It is always possible to do God's will.

Where Is Your Mind?

While I was trying to pray this morning my mind was turning over a disturbing conversation I had with a friend yesterday. Why couldn't she see the fallacy of her argument? Why couldn't I make myself clearer? If only I had pointed out such-and-such....

Then came the words of Colossians 3:1-2, about the place where *Christ* lives, "seated at the right hand of God." That is where our *minds* ought to live—just where He lives. "Let your thoughts dwell on that higher realm, not on this earthly life." What an order.

Does it mean I'm to become "so heavenly-minded I'm of no earthly use"? Quite the opposite. The more truly fixed my mind is on the level where nothing changes or deteriorates or disturbs, the more strength and serenity I will have to serve God and ordinary folks in "this earthly life."

Appropriating this fact by faith, I can commit all that was said and left unsaid yesterday, and the person who disturbed me, and lean my mind on the stillness of Christ in God.

Mercy Even There

In the story of *Pilgrim's Progress*, Christian meets Mr. Worldly Wise-man who tells him that there is not a more dangerous and troublesome way in the world than that to which Evangelist has directed him. There is a much easier road, he says, if he will only go to see a gentleman named Legality in the village of Morality. Christian, anxious to be rid of his heavy burden and tempted by the promise of a much more reasonable means of doing so, leaves the straight, narrow path and finds himself in worse trouble. There Evangelist finds him, and once more, Christian having repented of his foolishness, directs him back to the right road.

Who among us hasn't longed for a "safer" road, one not so fraught with difficulties? So we take some byway, and learn by sad experience that it is wrong. Yet even there the Lord's mercy waits for us, to remind us of His following love. "And the Lord provides even men who lose their way with pools to quench their thirst" (Ps. 84:6).

Drink, then, the water He gives. Receive His mercy, follow the instructions He will certainly send to put you back on the right road.

Thy Mighty Deeds

The psalms are full of exultation over the Lord's mighty acts, great deeds, fathomless thoughts (see, e.g., Ps. 92:4-5), yet often when we are praying for a mighty deed God's answer seems a feeble one. I have been asking Him for months for a miracle of grace: reconciliation of a divorced pair. A letter came from the woman telling of God's provision for her and her children, the kindness of people in the church, a job which she loves, simply "dropped in her lap." Evidences of grace at work, but not the big one I asked for.

Will we trust God for the accomplishment of His highest purposes, in spite of evil and suffering? Can we exult and praise and give thanks for whatever it takes to weave the "pattern for good" (Rom. 8:28, PHILLIPS)?

Lord, teach us to seek holiness above all things, in spite of all things, in the midst of all things. Then, if "solutions" are also possible in Your plan, give us faith for those as well.

Clouds and Mist

As a child I used to climb the White Mountains of New Hampshire with my father and brothers. We always tried to choose a perfect day—what we called a "real mountain day." Nothing dampened my spirits more than finding ourselves, halfway up the trail, enclosed in clouds and mist. It seemed to ruin the day. But of course we kept climbing, and usually broke out into sunshine as we neared the summit.

It would be nice to think that the Christian's ascent to glory would always be on "real mountain days," and never require going through any clouds. But such is not the way appointed. Mists rise, clouds lower, and we can't see a thing. The trail is obscured, the summit is gone, the valley we've come from might as well not exist. Reality disappears. The only reality left is mere vapor.

But here's a wonderful fact to latch on to: "Clouds and mist enfold him!" (Ps. 97:2). The Lord, the King of the mountains, is in the midst of us. Things invisible in the natural realm are visible to the eye of faith. Don't be misled or discouraged by mere vapor. Keep climbing. You'll see the Son when you reach the top.

I Can't Take It!

Some of us think this quite often, and some of us go right ahead and say it out loud: *I can't take it!* I've had more than enough of this, Lord—could You let me off the hook for awhile?

Timothy was a young minister who, Paul knew, would have to bear more than seems humanly bearable. "Now therefore, my son, take strength from the grace of God which is ours in Christ Jesus…. Take your share of hardship, like a good soldier of Christ Jesus" (2 Tim. 2:1, 4).

Whether you can take what life dishes out, and the difficult people life puts you into contact with, depends on what you take first. If you take from the grace of God the *strength* offered, you will find it absolutely sufficient to cover any need. You will find yourself quite amazingly able to bear the hardship of life's bitter battle as a good soldier. But the soldier has to be trained, prepared, and equipped first. Don't rush into the fray and try to "take it" without first taking strength.

Lord, for the needs or hardships of today, I come for Your strength. I receive it with thanks in Jesus' name. You, Lord, are my Strength.

When We Are Wronged

Psalm 109 is one of those called "imprecatory"—calling down terrible curses on those who do evil against the writer. It is not hard for me to identify with his expressions of outrage at the wrong. I know very well the human reaction to unfair judgment and false accusation. It is more difficult to understand the desire for *violent* retribution which the psalmist expresses so vividly. My temptation is to wish for vindication and at least an apology from the person who has wronged me. Neither may be forthcoming. What then?

"But thou, O Lord God, deal with *me* as befits thy honor" (v. 21).

That is certainly a safe prayer to pray! Leave the other to God, ask for whatever God wants to give or do in and to me, which will glorify Him, that "the greatness of Christ will shine out clearly in my person ... for to me life is Christ" (Phil. 1:20-21).

So High and So Low

We are prone to consider ourselves too busy (with important things, of course), too qualified (we have gifts, training, experience, responsibilities that few others have), too intelligent, to bother with small things. We exercise ourselves in matters too high for us, thus missing some of the "low" things God would teach us. Who are we, anyway? What is this pride of ours? Consider Him, "Who sets his throne so high but deigns to look down so low" (Ps. 113:6).

He who is truly great is never too great to give attention to the lowly. He "lifts the weak out of the dust and raises the poor from the dunghill" (v. 7).

This is what Love does. It never considers its own greatness or another's weakness. Forgetting itself, it gives freely, and gives and gives and gives again.

"The Powers That Be"

I did not realize that this was a biblical phrase, but it came at a needed moment. My husband and I have spent three weeks trying to fix up an old house. The list of things to be done is mostly of small improvements, but it seems that everything conspires to frustrate our schedule. Those frustrations look powerful to me. After a long conversation about what he considers necessary, now that our time is nearly up, and what I consider necessary (we see things differently, naturally!), I was nailed by these words in Psalm 119:23—"The powers that be sit scheming together against me; but I, thy servant, will study thy statutes."

"But Lord—I wanted to tear into six jobs to be done today!" (One of them, I confess, is preparation for a seminar tomorrow.)

"Are you *My* servant?"

"Yes, Lord."

"Are the powers 'that be,' that scheme against you, greater than I?"

"No, Lord."

"Then trust Me. And study (think about, read, ponder, heed) *My statutes.* You will find joy in them, rest for your soul, and the strength you need to cope with the necessary work."

What Will People Say?

I s there one of us who is not often troubled by that whisper, who is not tempted to allow it to control our decisions? It is a snare and a delusion. I do not mean that we should be heedless of the impression we may make on others who look to us as examples, or oblivious to godly warnings or advice. But when we have honestly sought to obey God and carefully searched His word for our cues, then we must not fear the consequences to our "image" or reputation. Turn all of *that* over to the only One "unto whom all hearts are open … and from whom no secrets are hid."

It is not the judgment of this world that finally counts. These words from Hebrews steady me:

Remember where you stand. You stand before Mt. Zion and the city of the living God, heavenly Jerusalem, before myriads of angels, the full concourse and assembly of the first-born citizens of heaven, and God the judge of all, and the spirits of good men made perfect, and Jesus the mediator…. The kingdom we are given is unshakable; let us therefore give thanks to God, and so worship him as he would be worshipped, with reverence and awe; for our God is a devouring fire.   HEBREWS 12:18, 22-24, 28-29

No Reservations

O bedience to the call of God must be wholehearted. That is, we can lay down no conditions, withhold no part of ourselves from Him.

"Show me the way that I must take; to thee I offer all my heart" (Ps. 143:8).

It is right and proper to ask for the Lord's clear direction about what to do, but it does not make sense to ask it if we offer only *some* of our heart. God will open a way for us when we open our hearts to Him.

Fiery Ordeals: Nothing Extraordinary

T here are certainly many different kinds of suffering and degrees of intensity, but the one we happen to be facing *now* always seems particularly severe. Never mind. Even if it is a fiery ordeal, Peter reminds us that there is nothing "extraordinary" about it. We often refer to the "mystery" of suffering and talk as though God has provided no clues whatsoever to His purposes—if He *has* a purpose. He has. And His book gives a number of clues. "It gives you a share in Christ's suffering, and that is cause for joy" (1 Pet. 4:13).

Is your suffering physical? Christ knows about that.

Has a friend betrayed you? Christ knows about that.

Did someone you love break your heart? Christ knows about that.

Have you suffered a serious loss? Christ knows about that.

Is it false accusation, misrepresentation, the refusal to believe in your love? Christ knows very well what *that* is like.

Then in all of these things, you enter a little bit deeper into the knowledge of Christ and the fellowship of His sufferings. What are those privileges worth to you? Be joyful, then! Be thankful! Alleluia!

Exert Yourself

Dietrich Bonhoeffer wrote of "cheap grace"—the distortion of Christianity that lays all the stress on free salvation and none on the fruits of salvation which show it to be genuine. The apostle Peter tells us we must try our hardest to supplement faith with virtue (see 2 Pet. 1:5). Virtue is a word often understood too narrowly. It covers a much wider area than sexual restraint. It means right action and right thinking.

Peter goes on to a list of necessary traits: knowledge, self-control, fortitude, piety (that means giving yourself to religious *duty*), brotherly kindness, and love. Just when we are about to gasp, "But that's an impossible list!" he tells us "These are *gifts.*"

"Oh. God will do it all!" we sigh.

However, *we* have to *do* something, too—possessing and fostering those gifts will keep us from being "either useless or barren in the knowledge of our Lord Jesus Christ. The man who lacks them is shortsighted and blind." That blindness is our own fault!

There is always work that only God can do—this is our salvation. We are helpless unless He helps us. But there is also work that we must do. It is hard work. It requires blood, sweat, toil, and tears. Study the lives of godly men and women. You will always find both the work of God in them, and their corresponding work, rigorous effort, exertion to "supplement their faith."

Intention

'Tell us, Fool! What is sin?' He answered, 'It is intention directed and turned away from the final Intention and Reason for which everything has been created by the Beloved'" (Ramon Lull, *The Book of the Lover and the Beloved* [New York: Paulist Press, 1978], 85).

This definition covers a great deal more ground than most of us like to allow. The heart's intention is known by God long before the deed is done. Even when we have "caught ourselves," and not done an evil thing, if it was in our hearts to do it we have sinned. Even when a deed may appear to be *good*, an evil intention sometimes lurks in the mind of the doer. What is sin. Jesus had scorching words for those who appeared to be religious but acted only out of pride: "White-washed tombs ... full of dead men's bones and all kinds of rottenness" (Matt. 23:27, PHILLIPS).

Purify the thoughts and intentions of my heart, Lord, and bring them into harmony with the Intention and Reason for which You have created everything—*Your* glory, *Your* pleasure.

I Will Bring You to Safety

T his morning as I was reading my Bible (the passage was 1 John, where there is much about light and love) many contradictory thoughts troubled me. Something painful has occurred. It causes confusion and doubt in my mind and has usurped my attention more often when I am trying to pray than anything else I can remember.

Suddenly I looked up and saw through the window the dark corner of the roof, laden with a thick quilt of snow. Beyond that was a hemlock tree, quietly waving in the wind, and through its black branches, shining in the dark blue of the early morning sky, was the clear sliver of the new moon.

Who made it all? I thought of Him, then, and the confusion fell away. He reminded me of His Word, "I have made you and I will bear the burden, I will carry you and bring you to safety" (Isa. 46:4).

A Good Beating

When I was a child I often heard the sound of rug-beating in the backyards of our neighbors. Vacuum cleaners were rare in those days. A sort of large wicker paddle was used to beat the dirt out of the rugs which were hung over the clothesline. Clouds of dust rose and blew away, and the clean rugs were lugged back into the house and laid on newly swept floors.

"A good beating purges the mind, and blows chasten the inmost being" (Prov. 20:30), says the Preacher.

We would probably prefer to skip passages such as this. We'd rather be comforted. But a verbal beating or a sudden emotional blow can have a very salutary effect on the spiritual life. The mind can get very dusty and cluttered. Nothing like a good beating to rid it of debris.

Cheer up! Do I think I didn't *deserve* it? Perhaps not, but I may rest assured that I *needed* it! Thank God for His faithfulness in permitting the blows I needed. Help *me*, Lord, to respond in faith, so that the beatings and blows will not be wasted.

Purge my mind, Lord.

Purify my heart.

Chasten my inmost being—that I may grow more Christlike.

The Accuser's Overthrow

One of Satan's favorite sports is archery. He aims his arrows with deadly accuracy at the bull's-eye of the human heart. One of those arrows is the reminder of past sins. No matter whether they are long since confessed and forgiven, he delights to accuse us anew: "Remember what you did to so-and-so? What about that night back in 1962? And do you imagine a holy God would ever really forgive and forget the way you...." And so it goes.

In the revelation of John we find the method whereby the saints overthrow the Accuser. It was *"by the sacrifice of the Lamb and by the word of God to which they bore witness"* (Rev. 12:11 NEB footnote).

The method will not be different in heaven than it is for us on earth. Nowhere, in heaven or earth or hell, is there power over Satan except in the blood of the Lamb and the Word of God. And no power or throne or dominion or authority anywhere in all the universe will ever overthrow the power of that sacrificial Lamb and that sacred Word.

> Midst flaming worlds in these arranged
> With joy shall I lift up my head!
>
> Nicolaus L. Zinzendorf

The Sense of Injured Merit

To every lover of the Lord, His adversary will be sure at some time to bring the temptation of a sense of injured merit. We find that when honors are distributed, or persons chosen for positions of leadership, we have been overlooked. Others whose qualifications, we believe, are distinctly inferior to our own, have advanced beyond us. Our merits have been ignored or belittled or discounted in some way. As soon as the thought occurs, it must be taken directly to Christ and submitted to His authority. He is, after all, our Judge and Master. To please *Him* is our aim—not to find recognition in the world.

What we do with this temptation—whether we try to vindicate ourselves, gain esteem, give way to bitterness, or whether we commit the matter quickly and quietly to God—reveals where our affections are really set. Are they directed toward things in heaven or things on earth?

Love—The Master Spring

William Wilberforce, the man responsible in England for the abolition of the slave trade, compared the love of God to a master spring, which "sets in motion and maintains in action all the complicated movements of the human soul. It soon settles all uncertain moral questions as to what is allowed" (William Wilberforce, *Real Christianity* [Sisters, Ore.: Multnomah Press, 1982], 84).

Reason asks what is the minimum requirement. Love asks how much it can offer. If we really love the Lord our God with all of our heart, soul, mind, and strength, motion and action will be transformed by love's power. Love outruns reason. Love brings down sophistries, excuses, and reservations. Love says, "Here, Lord, is all my heart. Do anything You want, at any cost. I am Your bondslave."

Where to Begin

To be transformed into the image of Christ, we must know His character, love His obedience to the will of the Father, and begin, step by step, day by day, to walk the same pathway. A very big order, we say. How shall we even begin? The answer is that we must begin where He began—with self-emptying. And how can we possibly do that? Why, at the Cross. There we are crucified—*with Christ*—and the sinful self is destroyed (see Rom. 6:6). What happens next? "If we ... died with Christ, we believe that we shall also come to life with him" (Rom. 6:8).

Help me, loving heavenly Father, to discover today the little humble ways in which I may "empty" myself for love's sake. Deliver me from the urge to give in to my own wants and wishes, that I may learn the joy of "coming to life" with You.

Lifestyle

T he word *lifestyle* has become a tricky and dangerous one for Christians, implying that an unlimited range of choices is open to us, from which we may select anything that happens to suit our fancy. We must remember first that the Incarnate Word entered into human life, "dwelt among us," and showed us glory, grace, and truth. We in turn, as those in whom Christ dwells now, are to live out His life wherever we are, whatever our gifts, temperament, or necessities. But this is what places a limitation on "lifestyle"—it is *His* life that we are to live. Paul's prayer for the Colossian Christians is "that your *manner of life* may be worthy of the Lord and entirely pleasing to Him" (Col. 1:10). This is to be our rule in the bedroom and kitchen; in the garden, shop, grocery store; in the office, the classroom, the subway, or on the ski slopes; whether we are old or young, sick or well, happy or sad, married or single, "advantaged" or "disadvantaged," First World or Third World. The "secret hidden for long ages" is to be revealed in and through *your* "lifestyle," *my* "lifestyle"—"the secret is this: Christ in you, the hope of a glory to come" (Col. 1:27).

What does He look like to those who watch you and me?

Such Cowards

T here is much emphasis today on empathizing with others' feelings, and on the candid confession or expression of those feelings. Jesus was "touched with the *feeling* of our infirmities" (Heb. 4:15, KJV). He was not a high priest, "unable to sympathize with our weaknesses" (Heb. 4:15). But we need to be reminded of what His *responses* were to people's feelings. For example, when the disciples panicked because a storm was sending waves right over the boat they were in, Jesus' first response to their desperate, "Save us, Lord, we're sinking!" was, "Why are you such cowards?" Cowardliness reveals faithlessness. "Why is it that you have no faith?" was Jesus' next question.

Medical science has discovered many connections between psychological stress and physical maladies. Fear is perhaps one of the most destructive emotions. The knowledge that Jesus is *in the boat* with us ought to put us at rest—even if waves are breaking right over us. Let's not be such cowards! Let's trust Him. He's got the whole world and even the wind, even the waves, even *my* problems—in His hand!

The Cross Is the Test of Love

Everything Jesus did in His life of obedience to the Father here in our world found its climax on the Cross. There, finally, He proved to the world of men how far He was prepared to go to rescue them. There He showed, once and for all, what love really means. There is no such thing as love that does not embrace suffering and self-sacrifice.

If we think we love someone, let us test that love by asking how far we are prepared to go for that person's sake.

If we imagine we love the Lord Christ, let us look at His broken and bleeding body hung up with nails and ask if what we call "love" has any of *that* quality in it. How much? How far will we go? What price will we pay? "Obedient unto death"—is that what *we* mean by love? It is what He meant. "Love one another as I have loved you," was His command (John 15:12).

Speaking the Truth in Love

One of the tests of love is the willingness to speak the truth when we know the truth will hurt. Preparation of heart is essential before we venture to do this. When the great apostle Paul went to the Christians at Corinth he confessed it was with weakness, nervousness, and trembling. Yet he went, "resolved that while I was with you I would think of nothing but Jesus Christ—Christ nailed to the cross" (1 Cor. 2:2).

We may bring that person first to the cross of Jesus, asking that the Spirit of God give us His eyes to see His heart to love, and "words found for us not by our human wisdom but by the Spirit" (1 Cor. 2:13).

Divine Dispossession

Jesus emptied Himself when He became a man. That Kenosis, or making Himself nothing, is a tremendous mystery which we will never fully comprehend, at least here on earth. But we are to follow Him in this—to be willing, for love of Him, to be utterly dispossessed. The process can take many forms, one of which Romano Guardini describes in connection with Jesus' radical cleansing of the temple.

"We sense the impotency of the spiritual act before the smiling unbelief of the world's mighty and wellborn" (*The Lord*, p. 36).

The Lord may be asking us to do something today for which we will need the willingness to be dispossessed. "Will it work?" we are wondering, and He simply says, "Never mind that. Do it." If, having obeyed, perhaps at some cost, we meet with smiling unbelief, or mere indifference, let us remember Jesus—willing to make Himself nothing, to be the butt of coarse jokes, hostility, pure scorn—for *us*. Looking at what He endured, maybe we will be able even to laugh at how small a thing our own humiliation is by comparison.

Lord, let me be your glad fool!

The Helplessness of God's Servants

One of the facts of Christian life that seems most inexplicable is God's not rescuing His most faithful and obedient servants from trouble. We know very well that He could, if He chose, commission a whole battalion of angels to protect us, or command a sea to split down the middle, or iron bars to disintegrate. Why does He sit up there, safe in His heaven, and do absolutely nothing?

Hold the question a minute. Why, when the greatest man besides Jesus, John the Baptist, came, did people fail to recognize him? Why did God let them "work their will upon him" (Matt. 17:12)? Why was the Son of Man Himself "given up into the power of men" (Matt. 17:22)? It is a picture of helplessness. Imagine—He who by His Word alone brought oceans, mountains, and suns into existence, was given up, handed over, made a present of—to wicked men.

Even the helplessness of God's servants is still under His control. He permits it. He does not tell us why when we want to know. He asks us to trust Him, to wait quietly and see His salvation—a far greater thing than a sudden rescue would have been.

But Lord—it's hard for us to wait. Help us, please. Give us the same patience and trust that You gave to John the Baptist and to Your Son.

The Supreme Act of Will

In the deep reaches of Eternity the Lord God determined to make a creature fully able to choose to love and obey. This meant that that creature—man—must be fully able also to deny his Maker and to disobey. Adam and Eve chose to disobey. Death entered the world then—separation from God the Creator and Source of Life. The self stands in opposition to Him—insisting, ever since that fateful choice in the Garden of Eden, *"My* will, not Thine." Christ became a man in order to die for man. He came to obey the Father's will. Thus when man lines himself up with Christ and says *"Not* my will," he makes the highest choice of which his God-given will is capable: he chooses to say no to himself. His own will is laid down voluntarily, and Christ's will is taken up. He may then say truthfully, "I have been crucified with Christ" (Gal. 2:20).

Every day of my life I am given opportunities for this supreme act of will. What joy to realize then that "it is God that worketh in me, both to will and to do of his good pleasure" (Phil. 2:13).

Lord of essential life, help me to die.
To will to die is one with highest life,
The mightiest act that to will's hand doth lie.

George MacDonald
Diary of an Old Soul, March 26

There Is No Other Way

To get to a place called Laity Lodge in Texas you have to drive into a riverbed. The road takes you down into a canyon and straight into the water. There is a sign at the water's edge which says, "Yes, you drive in the river."

One who has made up his mind to go to the uttermost with God will come to a place as unexpected and perhaps looking as impossible to travel as that river does. He may look around for an alternate route, but if he wants what God promises His faithful ones, he must go straight into the danger. *There is no other way.*

"I offer you the choice of life or death, blessing or curse. Choose life and then you and your descendants will live; love the Lord your God, obey Him and hold fast to Him: that is life for you" (Deut. 30:19-20).

When he takes the risk, he finds solid rock beneath him, and markers—evidence that someone has traveled this route before.

"The Lord your God will cross over at your head.... He will be with you, He will not fail you or forsake you. Do not be discouraged or afraid" (Deut. 31:3, 8).

Follow the Sign

When the road reaches the point of stoppage the traveler's attention is arrested. What to do now? Can it be right to plunge ahead *this* way? It certainly wasn't what I expected! But at the point of stoppage someone has anticipated my quandary and put up a sign. Shall I trust the sign? Shall I do what it says?

So in the walk of faith. At times we are brought to a dead stop. What next? Stand still and ask. "I am thy servant; give me insight to understand thy instruction" (Ps. 119:125). Instruction will come to God's servant. There will be something to obey, even if it seems a strange course.

> Trust and obey, for there's no other way
> To be happy in Jesus but to trust and obey.
>
> "Trust and Obey,"
John H. Samonis

Don't Get It Backwards

Be submissive ... to God. Stand up to the devil.

JAMES 4:7

Here is a command that only a man or woman who takes strength from God Himself can obey. The idea that submission is weakness is utterly false if that submission is to God or to those He has placed in authority. The weak submit to the devil (the line of least resistance for all of us fallen human beings) and stand up to God (easy for the children of Adam and Eve who started it).

Have you found that when there is a conflict between your will and God's, you are required to obey both of these commands—you can't obey one without the other? To choose submission to God is to choose defiance of His enemy and all he stands for. Beware of getting it backwards!

The Fire of His Grace

The refiner of silver has one object in mind: purity. There is a great deal of impurity that heat alone can destroy. Hence he sits and fans the fire, feeds it with fuel, watching until he can see his face in the silver.

The grace of God will tolerate nothing in us that obscures His own image. He insists (once we have asked that His will be done) on perfect purity. What means, then, do we expect Him to employ? What do we think we are asking for when we ask to become Christlike? Do we suppose there is a refining fire that is not very hot? Settle it once for all: God knows what He is doing. His object is good, acceptable, and perfect. Stay with Him. In His time your prayer will be answered.

"Lord, make my mirror-heart Thy shining place" (George MacDonald, *Diary of an Old Soul,* Oct.7).

Your Outward Life

The Old Testament tells us that man looks on the outward appearance, but God looks on the heart. We would surely find nothing there to argue about. Man looks on the outward because it's all he can see. But it is a revelation of what's inside. If this were not so, there would be no point in Paul's prayer for the Colossians, "that your outward lives, which men see, may bring credit to your Master's name" (Col. 1:10). Is there anything in your way of living that would indicate that you belong to a heavenly Master? If an outsider were to observe your "lifestyle" closely, listen to the way you speak, scrutinize the quality of your work, examine your response to pressure, what would he find? "Ah—*there's* one who's taking his cues from a different source than the rest of us!"

"We pray ... that you may bring joy to his heart by bearing genuine Christian fruit in all that you do" (Col. 1:10).

Fellow-Servants

As I begin a new day of work (which today happens to include not only my usual desk work and correspondence and housework, but sorting and putting away summer clothes and getting out winter ones, packing for a speaking trip, and preparing talks to be given) I am amazed to find that it is possible for me to join a company that includes the apostle John, angels, and prophets. Who, me? Yes. In the revelation of John, he tells how he fell in worship at the feet of the great angel who had shown him such astounding things (heaven wide-open, for example, and thrones and beasts and the bride of the Lamb). But the angel said, "No, not that! I am but a fellow-servant with you and your brothers the prophets and"—here is the category which may include you and me—"those who heed the words of this book" (Rev. 22:9). Every lover of the Lord may join that company.

God Will Stop at Nothing

In anguish of heart I cried to the Lord ... my cry reached His ears. The earth heaved and quaked.... He swept the skies aside.... He swooped on the wings of the wind.... The Lord thundered.... He shot forth lightening shafts.... He reached down from the height and took me" (Ps. 18:6-16).

There is no telling what terrific upheavals may be required to engineer the answer to one helpless person's prayer. We can see from this description (read all of Psalm 18) that Almighty God will stop at nothing. He will move heaven and earth to heave out of His way anything that might block His rescue operation. One thing we must remember: time is nothing to Him. Because it is everything to us, we quickly imagine that our prayers have come to nothing. Prayer never evaporates. It sets into motion forces as inexorable and perhaps as "unhurriable" as a glacier, but when the Lord's arm reaches down, no power in heaven or earth will frustrate Him.

Bend Your Necks to My Yoke

P eople often imagine that Christ offers the smooth working out of all life's difficulties. They are enticed by a
gospel of cheap grace—"God will replace my Volkswagen with
a Cadillac if I ask Him to, if I have enough faith," et cetera.
This view leaves out what matters most: Bend your necks to
My yoke. The "relief for your souls" which Jesus promises
comes only in accepting the burden He wants to bear with
you, not in dictating to Him what sort of fun you'd like to
have. Life always means burdens of one kind or another—it
isn't pure fun and games—but if you accept His choosing,
"your souls will find relief." His comforts come on His terms,
not on ours.

Praise to You, Lord, for your great and wise love.

The Test of Relinquishment

A braham had passed what would certainly seem two very
important exams long before this one—he had left his
country and followed God to a strange land, and he had
accepted the preposterous prediction that he would have a
child when he was a century old. But now came the Big One.
Would he make a sacrifice of that "only" son, the one he so
specially loved, the one through whom the promise of a great
nation was to come? How could he possibly slit that child's

throat? Abraham knew his God. He believed His word. He had faith in His character. He obeyed.

The untold blessing that would come was the result of Abraham's faithful obedience—his having relinquished what looked impossible to relinquish—to the God of the Impossible. "Because you have obeyed" (Gen. 22:18), unimaginable results took place.

We are so cocksure we know what will happen if we let go—of something, or somebody, some control, some possession, some dream, even some promise we believed was from the Lord. Here comes the Big Test. Will you open your fist? Can you trust the God of Abraham on this particular day in this year, in this matter He has put His finger on? What surprise of blessing may come *because you have not withheld it?*

Hidden Happenings

"M ay you know more and more of grace and peace as your knowledge of God and Jesus our Lord grows deeper" (2 Pet. 1:2, PHILLIPS).

There is an avocado pit suspended with toothpicks in a jar of water beside my kitchen sink. Days and weeks go by, and nothing whatever happens—or so it seems. If I knew nothing about the natural process of growth from a seed I would throw it away. It is slimy and ugly. Or, if I had great faith, I might ask God to give me an avocado tree tomorrow. As it is, I do neither. I only see that the water is supplied as needed. One day I notice the beginnings of a split. A week later (oh, *such* a slow business!) there are feeble white strings in the water and a strange sort of stick poking up from the split. One day the stick puts out slim little leaves. It is a tree! Not much of a tree, granted, but recognizable. It has a long way to go before there will be fruit.

So we must understand the secret process of spiritual growth. The beginnings are there with the very beginnings of faith, but the seed needs water. We must have the Water of Life. The knowledge of God is a process that goes on as we do what He says (see John 14:23). Then (slowly perhaps) fruit appears. If we wonder why we do not have as much grace and peace as we think we need, let us go on patiently doing what He tells us, learning to know Him, trusting that something is going on in the deep, hidden places which will surely produce fruit in God's time.

Have you wondered why a prayer you have prayed does nothing? Remember the avocado seed. The process was invisible for a long time. "Wait on the Lord ... and He shall strengthen thine heart" (Ps. 27:14, KJV).

This Ordinary Loneliness

Loneliness is one of the aspects of our human condition. There is nothing extraordinary about it. We flatter ourselves when we imagine that our troubles are unique and peculiar to our individual situation. They are unique and peculiar to the *human* situation. The Son of Man plumbed the very depths of loneliness when He came "out of the ivory palaces into a world of woe." Look up and away from yourself. Look up to the stars, which seem so remote, so pure, so untouched by suffering, so indifferent. The stars, too, belong to the same Lord who thoroughly understands our sense of aloneness.

"It is he who heals the broken in spirit and binds up their wounds, he who numbers the stars one by one and names them one and all" (Ps. 147:3-4).

How to Measure a Life

"Measure thy life ... not by the wine drunk but by the wine poured forth" (Ugo Bassi).

This sets the life of the true Christian in stark contrast to the life the world aims at. Giving, not getting, is the Christian's object.

Are you afraid you are missing out on something you thought you ought to have? Does the responsibility assigned to you get in the way of what you dream of doing, what "everybody else" is doing? Are you tempted to complain of interruptions or lack of time and money, so that your goals are frustrated? You need to examine your goals.

Wine drunk or wine poured forth—which matters most to you? Your answer may expose the superficiality of your understanding of what salvation is all about. Why did Christ die for us? Hear the word of the Lord: "His purpose in dying for all was that men while still in life [here, now] should cease to live for themselves, and should live for him who for their sake died" (2 Cor. 5:15).

A Hard Way and an Easy Yoke

These two sayings of Jesus seem to be in contradiction. "It is ... a hard road that leads to life" (Matt. 7:14, JB) and "My yoke is easy" (Matt. 11:28, JB). Perhaps we can understand the harmony of the two if we think of two dear friends hiking a mountain trail. The trail is steep and very rocky, and gets steeper and rockier the nearer it gets to the summit. The company of a friend does not make the distance shorter, but it makes it seem shorter. It doesn't eliminate any of the rocks, but the rocks don't seem so terribly daunting. The glad receiving of the yoke of Christ halves our life's burden. The road is still a tough one, but the roughness won't matter nearly so much.

Thank You, Jesus, for calling me into Your company.

Action as Opposed to Feeling

The instructions God gave to Israel through Moses covering their life in the wilderness were meant to teach them what it means to be His people. Things that "come naturally" are not to be the rule. They are to live not by material things or by the vicissitudes of changing human emotions but by the word of the Lord, spoken through His chosen servant.

"When you go into battle against an invader and you are hard pressed by him, you shall raise a cheer when the trumpets sound, and this will serve as a reminder of you before the Lord your God and you will be delivered from your enemies" (Num. 10:9).

Who responds to pressure with a cheer? None of us *naturally*. Our usual reaction would be a groan, not a cheer. What does it mean to be God's people? It means that we have an altogether different response than we formerly had. We have heard a Voice, we have seen the glory, we march to a new rhythm.

Be the Captain of my salvation, Lord, today—be in control of my responses. When I am pressed, let me obey Your word rather than my instincts. Teach me the joy of following my Captain.

Godliness With Contentment

It is one thing to bring our requests to God in prayer. We are told to do that (see Phil. 4:6). It is quite another to insist on something which has not been given, becoming nasty with God as though He were stingy and unloving. The people of Israel were roused to discontent by a "mixed company of strangers" who questioned them about the food God had supplied and reminded them of the good things they used to have in Egypt (fish, cucumbers, watermelons, leeks, onions, garlic) which He was no longer supplying.

Greed takes many subtle forms. Dissatisfaction with what God has given and complaints about the lack of what He has not given spring from a greedy heart. *This* house, *this* wife, *this* job, *this* talent, *this* achievement, *this* body—not what I really want. Give me *that* one. Do *that* for me—You did it for him, why not for me?

Lord, forgive my greed. You do love me. Forgive my doubting; help me to receive with thanksgiving Your supply of "daily bread," and to rest content with such things as I have. Your choices are perfectly wise. May I take them by faith, and happily.

Other Plans

T his thing that I wanted to do for You, Lord, I have not been allowed to do. I thought you had gifted me specially for this task—in other circumstances the gift has been obvious. It's needed here, it seems to me."

"Trust me, child, to make a way when the time comes. Trust me to open doors when I want you to serve me. Do not assume that the job is yours simply because you are good at it. I have other plans for you, plans which will open a way for you to learn to know Me. Is that not far better? Isn't that what you have asked for beyond all else?"

"Yes, Lord. Help my unbelief."

Take Up the Cross

What must I do to follow One who was crucified? Take up the Cross. What does that mean?

The "Cross" is every single thing, large or small, important in my eyes or trivial, in which the will of God cuts across my will—or my hopes, my preferences, my temperament, my tastes, my harmless whims. Each occasion offers me a choice. Will I go with Him (which means accepting the Cross) or will I accept the invitation of the enemies of Jesus: Come down from the Cross?

My choice reveals who I am: His faithful follower if I say yes to the chance to die, His enemy if I say no. I may save my life by voluntarily losing it, or I may lose it by insisting on saving it.

"Do you *want* to be My disciple?"

"Yes, Lord—with all my heart. Please help me not to miss the chances today brings to take up my Cross for Your sake."

Why This Sinking?

C hrist calls us to walk on water. That is what walking by faith means. The usual supports are gone, and we are beckoned by Him alone to get out of the boat, the "safe" place, and plant our feet firmly on what looks anything but firm. Like Peter, we are sometimes distracted, and we sink. If we do, shall we immediately conclude that it was a mistake to have gotten out of the boat? Was our guidance all wrong?

Be careful how you assign causes. Jesus did not rebuke Peter for *coming*. He rebuked him for *doubting*.

The Way of the Cross Leads to the Cross

E very work undertaken in obedience to a divine command, whether the work be that form of conflict with the powers of darkness that we call prayer, or whether it be the action that follows, leads sooner or later to a new demand on personal devotion to our Lord Jesus Christ."

So wrote Amy Carmichael in a small book privately printed for those who might be considering joining her Dohnavur Fellowship. For any who may read this now who might be considering following Christ *wherever* He may lead—do not forget (I have often forgotten and then been puzzled) that the Way of the Cross leads (always—we can depend on it) to the *Cross*. The Cross always tests the reality of our love. It makes "new demands in personal devotion."

How Much Is Enough?

The places where this question may be answered are Gethsemane and Calvary. I do not think we will get the answer we hoped for, but we will be shown how much is yet lacking in our love. Gethsemane revealed the Son's love for the Father. Calvary revealed His love for the world.

As long as there are ifs, buts, or conditions and limitations of any sort, we can be sure we know very little of loving God.

There is no help for me, Lord, but in Your everlasting love. Mine is a feeble frame, flickering, smoking, often extinguished. Forgive even the passing thought that perhaps I have loved You "enough."

> O may my love for Thee
> Pure, warm, and changeless be,
> A living fire.
>
> "My Faith Looks Up to Thee"
> Ray Palmer

Useless Weeping

The Lord, who notes the fall of every sparrow, notes also the fall of every tear. With some of those tears He sympathizes—those shed by His sowers who go forth weeping, bearing precious seed; those shed because of the world's rejection of His love. The tears that are the direct result of disobedience He notes and grieves over, but they cannot move

Him until they become the tears of honest repentance.

When Israel, convinced that God hated them and planned to let the Amorites defeat them (see Deut. 1:27), refused to go and fight, the Lord forbade them to enter the Promised Land. At this they wept. But their weeping was useless. He closed His ears to their pleas.

The God who is Love is not a God of soupy sentimentality. When prayer seems futile the cause may be our own rejection of some clear word of command. He will not disregard our freedom to choose.

Holy in Every Part

What happens today—let us be assured of this—is meant, in the purpose of our loving Father, to make us holy in every part. This making saints out of sinners is a lifelong business. One of the things that slow it down is our tendency to react to the happenings instead of responding to the Holder of the happenings. He is at work. He knows what He's doing. He asks us to believe in His thoroughly loving purpose.

"May God himself, the God of peace, make you holy in every part, and keep you sound in spirit, soul, and body, without fault when our Lord Jesus Christ comes. He who calls you is to be trusted; he will do it" (1 Thess. 5:23-24).

Dying We Still Live On

Sometimes life deals out troubles we feel sure we cannot survive. The routine disappointments, loneliness, losses, hungers, and pains which are simply a part of being human threaten at times to swamp us. So ... what else is new? Listen to Paul: "Distress, hardships, and dire straits; flogged, imprisoned, mobbed; overworked, sleepless, starving ... dying we still live on; disciplined by suffering ... we have always cause for joy ... we own the world" (2 Cor. 6:4-10).

Paul drew constantly from a deep well of strength not his own. That well is still brimful of pure water for any who know their need.

Drink today. The Christ-life in you will overcome those "dyings."

Stay Awake One Hour

When our Lord Jesus knew that the hour of His suffering was upon Him, He asked of the three chosen disciples only one thing—such a little thing: sit here and watch. They failed. Had they any inkling of the desperate flood-tide of anguish that was about to overwhelm their Master? Did they turn from it helplessly and take refuge in sleep, or were they so oblivious that they stretched out comfortably under the olive trees and took "forty winks" to kill time?

Jesus had asked for supportive companionship—three men

to count on. All they had to do was come into the garden, sit there while He prayed alone, and stay awake. It was a *share* in His sufferings. A very little share.

So He asks of us. Whatever the measure of suffering life has meted out, it is small indeed when measured against His—yet it is His call to fellowship. "Will *you* watch with me? Can you bear your weariness (your human trouble, whatever its kind) *with Me?*"

"Lord, I did not understand. I never dreamed You were asking *me* for something. I was preoccupied. I was oblivious. Here, Lord—my 'suffering' (this single hour of high privilege)—I offer it up. By Your grace, Your holy passion, let me watch with You."

Willing to Be Walked On

The word *humility* derives from the Latin *humus*, "earth." There is nothing apologetic about the earth. It is simply *there*—common, very low, and meant to be walked on.

"A man is never so proud as when striking an attitude of humility," wrote C.S. Lewis. Earth "strikes no attitudes"— that is, it draws no attention to itself, its commonness, its lowliness, its willingness to be walked on.

Pride seeks recognition.

Heavenly Father, we know that we have nothing that has not been given. Our very breath depends on Your ceaseless giving. Help us to learn genuine humility as we learn our utter dependence on You.

Strength for What's Coming

Y ou shall observe all that I command you this day, so that you may have strength to enter and occupy the land" (Deut. 11:8).

Moses has been reviewing what the Lord did for Israel— His discipline, His guidance, His protection. You know all this, He says. Now obey what He commands today. Then you'll have strength.

This was God's Word to me this morning, for I had wakened thinking of the ridiculously complicated agenda of the coming ten days. How did I get into this? Never mind that now. Just be obedient. Do today, faithfully, all that the Lord gives you to do. Then the strength will be given for what's coming. There is no need to go to pieces. Obey. Today.

Impossible Places

T he depressing tales people tell me, wherever I go, of the messes they are in, tempt me to doubt whether God has an answer. But doubt of His Word or His power is *always* from the enemy. There is no situation too hot, too tangled, too confining, too crushing, or too deep for the Lord our God to deal with.

"For thou, O God, hast put us to the proof and refined us like silver [a hot place to be]. Thou hast caught us in a net [a tangled place], thou hast bound our bodies fast [confining]; thou hast let men ride over our heads [uncomfortable, at least]. We went through fire and water, but thou hast brought us out into liberty" (Ps. 66:10-12).

While we are *in* the seemingly impossible place it does not look as though God has anything to do with it. He seems to be paying no attention whatsoever. Days, weeks, perhaps years go by without deliverance. Do not stop trusting. The process of refining silver takes time as well as heat. He is in control of the process, never for a moment forgetting the one who feels forgotten. There will be an end and a deliverance and freedom—according to the perfect chronology of Him who loves us with an everlasting love.

O Patient Refiner, help us patiently to accept Your refining, joyfully to expect the fulfillment of Your shining purpose.

The Greed of Doing

When Satan came to tempt Jesus in the wilderness his bait was intended to inspire in the Lord the lust to do more than the Father meant for Him to do—to go farther, demonstrate more power, act more dramatically. So the enemy comes to us in these days of frantic *doing*. We are summoned ceaselessly to activities—social, political, educational, athletic, spiritual. Our "self-image" (deplorable word) is dependent not on the quiet and hidden "Do this for My sake" but on the list the world hands us of what is "important." It is an outrageously unreasonable list, and if we fall for it we neglect first things: sitting in silence with the Master, to begin with. Then God-given work—being husband or wife, father or mother, *spiritual* father or mother to those nearby who need protection and care; hidden work, often which is never on the world's list because it lends nothing impressive to one's dossier.

> O Master, let me walk with Thee
> In *lowly* paths of service free…
>
> Washington Gladden

May I accept with joy the work You have given me, Lord. Deliver me from the greed of doing more than You mean me to do, for Jesus' sake.

The Greed of Being

The Snake in the Garden struck at Eve with the promise that she could be something which had not been given. The Lord the Creator designed her to be first *human,* then woman. If she would eat the fruit forbidden to her, she could "upgrade her lifestyle"—she could become like God. She inferred that this was her right, and that God meant to cheat her out of it. The way to get her "right" was to disobey Him. Very simple. Very quick.

No new temptations ever come to any of us. Satan has no new tricks. He doesn't need any. The same old tricks work very well today, although under different guises. When there is a deep restlessness for which we find no explanation it may be due to the greedy desire to be what our loving Father never meant us to be. Peace lies in the trusting acceptance of His design, His gifts, His appointment of place, position, capacity. It was thus that the Son of Man came to earth—embracing all that the Father willed Him to be, usurping nothing that was not given.

"Lo, I come ... to do Thy will, O God."

The Greed of Having

When "a mixed company of strangers" joined the Israelites the people began to be greedy for better things (see Num. 11:4). God had given them exactly what they needed in the wilderness: Manna. It was always enough and always fresh. Furthermore it was good—it tasted like butter-cakes. But the people lusted for variety. These strangers put ideas in their heads—"There's more to life than *this* stuff! Is *this* all you've got? You can have more. You gotta *live* a little!"

So the insistence to have it all took hold on God's people and they began to wail, "all of them in their families at the opening of their tents" (v. 10).

There is no end to spending, getting, having. We are insa-tiable consumers, dead set on competing, "upgrading," show-ing off ("if you've got it, flaunt it"). We simply cannot bear to miss something others deem important. So the world ruins the peace and simplicity God would give us. Contentment with what He has chosen for us goes, along with godliness. Instead of giving thanks, we wail—and we teach our children to wail.

From all greed for things not needed, Good Lord, deliver

us. Teach us to rest quietly in Your promise to supply and to realize that if we don't have it we don't need it.

What About Him, Lord?

L oving God means doing what He says. One of the distractions the enemy often uses to steer us away from loving Him purely is what others are doing or not doing. Sometimes those others are our responsibility. God holds us accountable for what they do. Most of the time, however, they are God's business, not ours. He is asking for our undivided attention—a heart *united,* a *single* eye, a will bent on obedience regardless of what others may be up to.

When Peter had three times asserted his love for Jesus in that lovely lakeshore breakfast scene he was distracted immediately by the sight of another disciple (an especially beloved disciple).

"Lord, what will happen to him?"

"If it should be my will that he wait until I come, what is it to you? Follow me" (John 21:21-22).

This is His Word to us when there is nothing we can or should do about the way other disciples are following.

A No Is a Mercy

Prayer establishes a relationship between God and His child. An earthly father, because of his responsible love for the little one, says yes to some requests and no to others. So God does. Think back to childhood. What if our fathers had given us exactly what we asked for when we asked? What sort of adolescents would we have become? What sort of adults?

Thank God He loves us purely. He has often, therefore, said a strong, infinitely *loving*, No. Thank Him for that. He may say yes to a foolish prayer—as the father of the prodigal did—but that answer will give us a hard lesson, and ultimately drive us back to Him with a new understanding of what our relation to Him was intended to be in the first place.

"I have loved thee with an everlasting love: therefore with great mercies have I drawn thee" (Jer. 31:3). God's "No's" were some of those great mercies.

The Heart of Our Need

As having nothing, and *yet* possessing all things" (2 Cor. 6:10, KJV).

Nothing makes the one who has no faith more jubilant than seeing one who has faith fail to receive what he asks God for. And nothing is more disappointing to the asker if he does not yet truly believe in the absolute love of God.

When prayer is not answered according to our idea of "answered"—in other words, when we don't get the thing we *meant*—God is calling us to a far deeper knowledge of His character. In what sense does His child "possess all things"? Why, in being *His* child! We are Christ's and Christ is God's (see 1 Cor. 3:23), therefore we own the world!

We are being drawn deep into the heart of our need, which we did not clearly understand, when we asked for the thing not given. Our Father understands it perfectly and gives what is, for us, now, immeasurably *better*.

"Do you believe Me, my child?"
"Lord, I believe. Help Thou mine unbelief."

More Important Than Happiness

Prayer for others is a way of laying down our lives for them—in other words, of doing what Christ did, accepting with His whole heart, soul, and *life* the holy and perfect will of the Father. The people I care most about are those whose lives most affect mine—whose sorrows are my sorrows, whose joys are my joys. It follows, then, that my prayers for them are likely to become prayers for myself—selfish prayers. "What will God's answer *do* to *me*?"

It is a deep lesson the work of Christ on earth teaches us, if we will learn of Him: a person's faith in God is infinitely more important than his health or his success or his happiness. We must ask for whatever will lead our loved ones to believe—not in some neat notion of good, but in Him who is the Origin of all good, the Father of Lights.

Holy God, make us, make them, holy.

Gifts We Never Thought of Asking For

If God granted us *only* what we asked for we would be dead in a second. Our very breath is an un-asked-for gift of grace. The power to move my pen—on how many un-asked-for faculties does it depend? On my brain for one thing, which at this moment is functioning. At this moment I am awake and not asleep; sane and not insane; warm and well, not cold and sick; free to write; free to choose; free from prison chains and the terrible bondage of drink, drugs, or hatred. I have a brain and a hand and a pen and a notebook and a place to sit comfortably and the ability to write cursive script and the knowledge of language and the Book of Books, which is the source of my knowledge of God. I have His Holy Spirit, who breathes into my nostrils the breath of life and illumines my mind to understand and strengthens my heart to obey.

Did I ask for all of those things?

Solomon's prayer in 1 Kings 8 showed me afresh that most of the blessings and gifts of God—millions and millions of them—come unasked. Solomon asked for many specific things but he left out most of what we all need all the time. God *loves* all the time. God *knows* what we need and God *gives*— whether we ask Him or not and whether we love Him or not, or even give Him a single thought per year. Is it not time to say thank You?

As the Need Arises Day by Day

T he Lord our God be with us.... May he never leave us nor forsake us ... and may the words of my supplication to the Lord be with the Lord our God day and night, that, as the need arises day by day he may grant justice to his servant" (1 Kings 8:57-59)

When we make our prayers to God we leave out most of what we need—first because we take almost everything basic and essential for granted, and second because we are ignorant. But our Father knows. We forget the prayer; He remembers. We can leave responsibility in His hands, expecting that *as the need arises* He will know what to do. He wants us to learn where good comes from, for the Father's heart yearns for the son's response. The God of the Universe, we might say, "strains His ear" to catch the least whisper of supplication and, if it may be, of gratitude. If we have *prayed* for something, *sometimes* we remember that it was God who gave it to us. And sometimes we gladden Him with a grateful word. Why not keep a little notebook, recording prayers asked and answered? It strengthens faith.

Love Takes Authority

How was Jesus able to live without the least adulteration of selfishness in His life on earth? The answer is love. He loved the Father purely. His all-consuming love brought Him "Out of the ivory palaces into a world of woe—Only His great, eternal love made my Savior go" (Henry Barraclough). His love kept Him here. Obedience, the daily practical outworking of that love, was the routine of His life. Because He loved the Father He loved us, and gave Himself for us. Love took authority over self in the life and death of Christ.

We claim to be His followers. How shall we behave? What will be the routine? Will it be love? Will it be thanksgiving? Or the opposite?

John Newton's magnificent old hymn "Glorious Things of Thee are Spoken" ends with these lines:

> 'Tis His love His people raises,
> over self to reign as kings,
> And as priests His solemn praises
> Each for a thank-offering brings.

Lord, lift us by the power of Your love to the place of authority over every manifestation of the self. Free us from its rule, that we may serve the King of Kings with the daily offering of gratitude.

Misgivings

"Test me, and understand my misgivings," the psalmist prayed (Ps. 139:23).

It is a great comfort to know that He to whom all hearts are an open book is the One who accurately tests *and* understands. Lately I have had a whole set of misgivings about some people I have been praying for. I am aware of the lack of faith that allows such doubts, yet to bring them all, along with my ignorance and faithlessness, to Him who thoroughly understands them, is rest indeed.

When the great prophet Elijah had just seen the miracle of the holy fire, demonstrating his God's reality and power, he panicked because of a woman's threats, and fled. There the Lord met him, understood his misgivings, provided—not rebuke or punishment—but food and water and sleep. What tender mercy!

So He probes my heart, diagnoses its need, provides succor exactly according to the nature of the malady. I have a most loving Lord.

Something to Give Back

One who had suffered a great loss was questioned repeatedly about his response. "Were you not bitter? Not angry at God for taking away what was so precious to you?" Each time, although he understood the sympathy out of which the question sprang, his answer was the same: No, he was not bitter. First, because there was never the slightest doubt in his heart or mind that God loved him still and had "in faithfulness ... afflicted" him (Ps 119:75, KJV). Second, he saw that it was by His own gifts of grace that he possessed something to give back to the Giver. It was not something that cost him nothing—it had cost him, it seemed at the time, quite literally ALL.

"Go and sell what you have," Jesus said to the rich young man, "and come follow me" (Matt. 19:21). Sadly, the man, not realizing the precious privilege being offered to him in that invitation, saw only the loss of what he prized most. Had he had eyes to see through the visible, he would have poured out the paltry pile at once.

"Let it go," says Jesus to each of us today. "Give it up to Me as I gave My all for you. You will not be sorry. I promise you, you will not be sorry."

God's Curriculum

My prayers today for three people seemed, to my small faith, too much to ask. For one, I asked healing of a malady for which modern medical science has no cure. For another, release from "the body of this death." For the third, deliverance from what may turn into a legal mess. Were such prayers wrong? If so, it would not be because they were too *big* for Him to whom nothing is impossible. When I wondered if they were, the words of a hymn came immediately to mind:

> Thou art coming to a King—
> Large petition with thee bring,
> For His grace and power are such,
> None can ever ask too much.
>
> From "Come, My Soul, Thy Suit Prepare"
> by John Newton

My prayers may be mistaken for another reason: perhaps I am asking God to waive, for these three people whom I love, the requirements for the degree they seek: an A.U.G.— "Approved unto God." Their circumstances may be the very curriculum God has selected to qualify them for that highest of all degrees. Would I want them to settle for any other? Am I asking that they be allowed to cut classes? Do I want the Lord to grant them the degree without the rigors of the required course?

Their circumstances (and mine, today) are God's curriculum. Only He knows when we have fulfilled the requirements. In the meantime may we *study* to show ourselves approved unto God.

How to Go On

The mother of seven children lost her husband and was robbed by a very clever lawyer of all that the husband had left her. Few of her family or friends came to the funeral.

Brokenhearted and penniless, she returned to the house from the cemetery, went into the kitchen, and picked up her broom.

"I shall never forget the comfort of that soft *whisk, whisk* in the kitchen. Mother's broom spoke to me: 'We will go on.'"

An old black man sat in a doctor's office with his daughter. *Cancer* was the word they had just heard. They were very quiet for a moment.

"Can you ..." the daughter began.

"There is nothing we can do. It has gone too far," was the doctor's reply.

Silence again. Then, very quietly, the old man said, "We jist gonna go right on."

"Sure we will," said the woman.

It was not the end of the world, and it certainly was not the end of the lovingkindness and tender mercies of the Lord who loved them and was not taken by surprise. He would be there. He would carry them as a father carries his child (see Deut. 1:31). They did not see the way ahead. They saw only what they were to do at once.

Duty is ours. Events are God's. There is *always* something we can do. Pick up the broom. Do our regular work.

Leave to thy God to order and provide;
In every change He faithful will remain.

Katharina Von Schlegel

All That Comes to Me

The Orthodox Morning Prayer includes this petition: "Teach me to treat all that comes to me throughout the day with peace of soul and with firm conviction that Your will governs all."

I had thought of "all that comes to me" as coming from outside, in other words, from the action of others. Today what came was the sudden sickening realization that I had forgotten a speaking engagement last night. (It was on my calendar but not in my engagement book. I had looked only at the latter.) I did not treat this with peace of soul. The pastor was very gracious when I called. "God is in control," was his word of comfort. Yes. He is still there in spite of my inexcusable failures. What destroyed my peace was not merely the thought of those I had sinned against—their inconvenience, disappointment, offense—but the thought of *my reputation* for faithfulness. I had to confess that subtle form of pride.

Nothing that comes to me is devoid of divine purpose. In seeking to see the whole with God's eyes, we can find the peace which human events so often destroy.

I rest, dear Lord, in the knowledge that You are the Blessed Controller of all things.

Reckoned Among Transgressors

One of the "little deaths" we are asked to die, if we are truly following Christ, is to be blamed for something we did not do. It is by no means always possible to prove our innocence, and, for the servant of the Lord, it is often both unwise and unnecessary even to attempt to prove it. Never mind. He has been over that course Himself—far more painfully than we can imagine, because, unlike us, He was thoroughly pure, wholly blameless in the farthest recesses of His holy heart. Our accusers will have little difficulty finding valid reasons to blame us if we manage to clear ourselves of one thing or another. Why not simply rejoice in being permitted, for Christ's sake, to be reckoned among transgressors—in this one particular? It is a *share* (though a very small one) in His sufferings.

Help me, Lord, to move toward knowing *You*, toward a deeper fellowship in the mystery of Your suffering which was—let me not overlook this—not only for my accusers but for *me*.

Convenient Obstacles

When Jesus asked the paralytic at the Pool of Bethesda if he wanted to be healed it was not because the *need* for healing was not obvious. Instead of answering the question, the man presented excuses—"I have no one to help me.

Somebody always beats me to it." In thirty-eight years he had become rather comfortable with his helplessness. It freed him of all effort and responsibility.

It is convenient for some of us who are physically fit to lie on our familiar pallet of excuses while others bustle around us, doing what we ought to be doing. If the possibility of change is offered, we decline. It would mean the loss of our right to indolence.

Sometimes, as in the case of this man, the Lord does not wait for our consent. In His mercy He heals us anyway—that is, He deprives us of the chance to be thoroughly, helplessly selfish. Then, like it or not, we must get up and start doing His will. Then we learn freedom we never dreamed of—the glorious liberty of obedience.

Heaven-Sent Obstacles

Therefore I will block her road with thorn-bushes and obstruct her path with a wall, so that she can no longer follow her old ways" (Hos. 2:6)

God is comparing the unfaithfulness of Israel His bride to a harlot. Whenever we stray from the path He has marked for us we are like that wayward woman. So, in His mercy, He blocks the byway with a hedge of thorns. We are stopped in our tracks, bewildered, wondering *Why*. Why, when things seemed to be going so well, this sudden obstruction, this impassable barrier to prayers? Although it does not in any way appear to be so at the time, it is in reality a gift of grace. To proceed further along that road would mean destruction. In His love the Lord stops us—*in His love.*

Father, teach me to see Your love at work in what looks to me like dead ends. You are both Alpha and Omega, Beginning and End. Thank You for standing in the way.

Trouble Is Only a Gateway

God took the very disobedience of the "harlot" Israel and made it over anew. This is the great message of salvation—not that we shall be protected from the woes that all men suffer in this spoiled world, but that the woes themselves are subject to transformation. When Israel, the Bride, had gone whoring she had to be punished—but then the Bridegroom wooed her all over again, went with her into the wilderness, comforted her who deserved to suffer, restored her vineyards, made her fruitful again, and turned "the Vale of Trouble into the Gate of Hope" (Hos. 2:15).

Something I am "going through" today looks like a rough valley. It is not only that. It is, in the hand of God, a way out, a passage to a better place, a gateway to glory. Shall I drag my feet and postpone arrival? Lord, help me to skip gaily!

Equality—Something to Be Coveted?

The first protest for equality occurred, as did all subsequent protests, because someone could not abide another's position of authority. It was at Hazeroth, when Miriam and Aaron began to speak against their brother Moses. The first charge, that he had married a Cushite woman, was not the real issue. "Is Moses the only one with whom the Lord has spoken? Has he not spoken with us as well?" (Num. 12:1-2). In other words, who did he think he was? After all, Miriam had watched over Moses when he was only a baby in a basket. That he should be in a place of authority over her was not to be borne. She was punished for her protest—turned into a leper.

Here is the great lesson of this story: her healing came through the prayers of the one she had criticized. We never know the importance of the place God has assigned to another—how our own well-being may depend on His having given it to that person rather than to us. Conversely, when we are criticized for doing a job given to us by God, do we think of praying for the critic? Perhaps my position—one that exposes me to bitter jibes and false judgments—is a specially privileged position for prayer.

Grant me grace, Lord, to surrender all judgments of the motives of others to Your all-seeing wisdom. Strengthen me to keep my mouth shut and remember that You are in perfect control of all things. And help me to pray, especially to pray for those who despitefully use me. For Jesus' sake. Amen.

Seek Things That Last

The world and the gifts it prizes can be bought with money. Christ and His gifts are priceless. Everything that happens is meant, in the loving purpose of Him who paid for us with blood, to wean us *away* from the world and to Himself, to disenchant us with temporal things and enchant us with heavenly, to feed us with Living Bread, not with stones. As soon as we attach our ambitions to things that will let us down He calls us in some specific way to let go of such handholds and take hold of Him. He and He alone is able to keep us from falling, able to fill the empty places the world is always clamoring to fill.

Lord, by all Your dealings with me today, may I be drawn a little farther from the love of things which are seen and a little nearer to the love of things which are not seen, things which can never be corrupted. Pull me hard, Lord, to Yourself.

Do I Love My Neighbor?

If I imagine that I love my neighbor let me test my love by asking how glad I am that he has achieved what I have failed to achieve; that he has managed to acquire what I have long wished to acquire; that he is loved by someone or by many or in some way that has never been granted to me. Do I rejoice because he has reasons to rejoice that have been denied me? Can I honestly praise God for His goodness to my neighbor? Can I praise Him wholeheartedly for His gifts to me?

If I love my neighbor *as myself* there will be no reason at all for the least twinge of jealousy—because I will be just as happy that *he* has what I wanted as I would be if *I* had it.

Help me, heavenly Father, to beware of making claims of love for You unless my love for my neighbor can pass this test.

Look for the Ancient Paths

Whenever we reach an intersection in our journey of life some decision is required. Stop. God is calling us to faith—that is, to choose to do His will. How shall we know what that is?

The prophet Jeremiah was writing to a people stubborn and determined to go their own way regardless of God's many warnings and directions.

"Stop at the cross-roads; look for the ancient paths; ask, 'Where is the way that leads to what is good?' Then take that way, and you will find rest for yourselves" (Jer. 6:16).

Look for the *ancient* paths—God's ways, often scorned as mere tradition. We often prefer to go our own way, or to follow whatever is new and different and exciting.

God calls us, not to novelty but to what is good. To choose that road means a radical departure from the "way that seems right to man" (Prov. 14:12)—the beaten path, the wide highway—a stern rejection of whatever deters us from the pure and the holy. But the ancient way, rejected by the crowd, leads to *rest*. The loving-kindness of our Guide draws us always to the place of relief from stress, release from things that weigh us down, refreshment for our tiredness.

"Then take that way."

Sudden Change

Suddenly it happens that a source of life or joy or refreshment is cut off. The supply dries up and we panic—"What shall I do *now?*" The panic results from our habit of expecting people and circumstances to operate according to our wishes. When they change, the heat is turned on, drought is imminent, and unless we remember the single unfailing Source of Life, we shrivel.

The father of a young family, for example, faces the loss of his job; a woman long active in serving others for the Lord has to learn to be served; a girl is abandoned by the man who was about to marry her; a hard-pressed student fails to make the grade that will qualify him for a scholarship. Where to turn?

"Blessed is the man who trusts in the Lord, and rests his confidence upon him. He shall be like a tree ... that stretches its roots along the stream. When the heat comes it has nothing to fear;... In a year of drought it feels no care and does not cease to bear fruit" (Jer. 17:7-8).

Scriptural Weight Lifting

The weight of the cares that are laid on us is meticulously measured by the one who "knows our frame" and "knows full well that we are dust" (Ps. 103:14). Not a hair's weight more than we can sustain will be added to the load, but a load there must be for each of us, for we are in training.

We are promised something intriguing and mysterious when this is all over—"an eternal weight of glory, out of all proportion to our pain" (2 Cor. 4:17). What will it be? Who can say or even imagine? *Glory* is all we know—a heavy mass of something far too wonderful to explain in human terms. We must be *trained* to bear it—it cannot be borne *there* unless we are disciplined *here* by suffering. Today's sorrow has everything to do with tomorrow's joy, though the joy will be *out of all proportion* to the sorrow.

Heavenly Trainer, teach me to lift the little weight You lay on me today. Teach me to hold it steadily and gladly, developing spiritual muscle in anticipation of the great load of glory You are saving for me.

Very Thoroughly Initiated

This is Paul's expression when he was in prison: "I have been very thoroughly initiated into the human lot with all its ups and downs" (Phil. 4:12).

For a family I love very much the present time is one of the "downs." I would give anything to be able to shield them from the hard experiences, but am reminded by these words that this is an essential element of the initiation process; to be brought low, as well as to have plenty. In the same paragraph Paul mentions contentment, and strength. My prayers, therefore, must take into account first of all God's purpose in what is happening: a thorough initiation, that they may be mature disciples.

I cannot ask, Lord, for exemption for them. But I do ask You to give, in the midst of the rigors, joy, contentment, and strength. I count on Your unbreakable promises.

A Castle Besieged

In one way or another we sometimes fear that our defenses are crumbling. What happens to the soul at such a time depends on the soul's habit of defense.

> Did we in our own strength confide, Our striving would be losing; Were not the right Man on our side, the Man of God's own choosing: Dost ask who that may be? Christ Jesus, it is He; Lord Sabaoth His Name, From age to age the same, And He must win the battle.
>
> Martin Luther

Samuel Rutherford wrote, "The soul is a castle that may be besieged but cannot be taken" (*Letters* [Chicago: Moody Press], 92). When besieged, we may name the Name that is a

Strong Tower. The man of faith runs to that Tower, not to any other (the towers of pride, independence, bitterness, self-vindication, retaliation, despair, self-pity, or fear). There he is safe. Besieged, yes. Taken, no.

The Power, the Glory, and the Humbling

∞

The disciples had just been given the vision of Christ's glory in the transfiguration and seen the miracle of deliverance of a demon-possessed boy. It was a real crowd-pleaser. They were "struck with awe at the majesty of God" (Luke 9:43). Jesus turned from this admiration to His disciples, telling them He had something to say just to them:

"The Son of Man is to be given up into the power of men" (v. 44). His dazzling glory on the hill, the demonstration of authority over the spirit world—no protection there from the ignominy of being put into men's hands. He did it for God. He bore it in perfect union with the will of the Father for the sake of the world.

And what about us who want to be faithful followers? Shall we expect power and glory without suffering and shame? If God leads us into a victim situation should we be surprised? He will let us suffer at the hands of other people; He will let us be powerless at times. It is then the word comes to us which was not spoken to the admiring crowds: The Son of Man is to be given up....

"Will you, when you find yourself at the mercy of unkind,

thoughtless, or even cruel people, take it for Me?" He asks. "I know your suffering. I took it for you. I am with you in it today."

What We Do Not Want

In the life of each of us there are things we do not want. "Oh, to be rid of *that!*" is our sigh. We may seek ways to be rid of it (or her or him), only to have our plans fall through, or it may be very obvious that there is no possible way to make it vanish, not now, not here. What shall we do? Go to the hidden place with God. Be honest with Him about your desire. There is no use trying to evade the truth with Him to whom the deepest places of the heart are as visible as is the sun to us. Tell Him the truth, confess the wrong that may be revealed in the light of His Word, and ask humbly what He wants you to do. Is there a way to change things? He will show you how. Does God not want them changed? Then—count on it—He wants acceptance. He wants you to believe in His power to do the very best ("*I* have made, and *I* will bear, even *I* will carry"). He will give all the grace you need, if you'll receive it.

"But it wasn't grace I wanted. I wanted the removal of the problem."

"Look, child—I have something better than your dreams in store for you. This is a little part of your growing big enough to receive it. Will you believe Me?"

Who—Me, Lord?

Gideon said, in effect, to the angel of the Lord, "You've picked the wrong man—I belong to the weakest clan, I'm the low man on my father's totem pole. How can *I* do a job like this?"

Not Moses, not Jeremiah, not Gideon, not you or I. The imperative is outside and beyond us, larger than our estimates, usually quite out of harmony with the "me" we foster and fondle. The divine idea of who we are is a shock. We recoil from it, we remind God that He must have made a mistake this time.

"The Lord answered, 'I will be with you, and you shall lay low all Midian as one man'" (Judg. 6:16).

Reread that promise, emphasizing the word *you*. It is *you* I have called, it is *you* I will unfailingly accompany, it is *you* who will do this job for Me. Remember My promise, "I will be with you. I will help you."

The Mightiest Act

There will be one or two things today that we would not have put on our plates if the will of God were merely a smorgasbord. It is not a smorgasbord. The plate is served to us—our "daily bread."

What am I to do, then? Recognize that all that is not according to my tastes and preference provides an opportunity for "the mightiest act that to will's hand doth lie" (George MacDonald, *Diary of an Old Soul*)—that is to will to die. Each time I will to accept or to do what I would not have chosen, provided I accept or do it for the sake of Him who loves me, I move a little more toward that essential life—the life which *is* Christ. "For to me, life is Christ, and death gain" (Phil. 1:21).

Relinquish Everything

Why did crowds follow Jesus? He said it was their desire to have something—loaves, fishes, healing. They did not begin to comprehend what He would ask of *them* if they wanted to become disciples. They must relinquish not only evil and defiling things, but all of the very best: father, mother, wife, children, brothers, sisters, for a start. In addition, life itself, and everything they possessed. What would that leave? Nothing whatever, as the world counts things. But they would possess what the world never counts—Christ Himself, and, possessing Him, they would have all. "All things are yours, for you are Christ's, and Christ is God's."

Master and Lord, teach me to value what You value, to love what You love.

Deal First With God

It is modern man's habit to speak much of his troubles (which he generally calls *problems*). Endless time and energy are expended on "sharing" when prayer is really what is needed. Hannah's strength lay in her habit of taking things first to God. In her grief over her childlessness she wept and could not eat, but when Elkanah asked what her trouble was there is no record of her telling him. He guessed it, as a loving and understanding husband may, but Hannah *stood before the Lord* and prayed to Him, weeping bitterly. Eli the priest saw her lips moving in silent prayer and took her for a drunk. She explained that she was pouring out her heart before the Lord—but she did not say why. She did not think it necessary to pour her heart out to the priest. Nor did he inquire. He simply asked God to answer her.

The lessons of prayer are deep. We will not learn them until we form the habit of dealing first directly with God. Usually we will find we need not bother husbands, priests, or other busy people who have burdens enough to bear. We will be free to bear others' burdens, which we are commanded to do. We are also told to bear our own. Nowhere are we told to lay our burdens on others, or to oblige them to bear ours.

The Strength of the Lamb

When the Philistines marched against Israel at Mizpah, Israel was terrified and implored Samuel to intercede for them. He offered up a suckling lamb and prayed out loud. While this was going on the Philistine forces were bearing down on them (see 1 Sam. 7:10).

So it is when powers of evil seem about to overtake the Christian. Those powers seem tremendous when we have no opposing strength of our own. The Philistines had physical strength. Samuel had only the little lamb and prayer—spiritual resources that seemed feeble indeed against such an onslaught. But when he laid hold of those resources the Lord thundered.

We have access to spiritual forces infinitely greater than those which oppose us. The "accuser of the brothers," Satan, is always very busy, but will ultimately be vanquished—"By the sacrifice of the Lamb they have conquered him" (Rev. 12:11).

We face opposition (today, perhaps?) and it appears that visible forces are victorious over the spiritual. Let us lay hold in faith on the strength of the Lamb of God and the promised efficacy of prayer. The Lord's "thunder"—His intervention—may not be audible to us. It may seem that He does nothing at all (the "brothers" of Revelation had had to lay down their lives)—but the "hour of victory for our God, the hour of His sovereignty and power" is on its way. As we identify ourselves in faith with the perfect offering of God's Lamb, the Power of the Blood is ours to overcome. Never mistake appearances (physical forces) for Reality (spiritual ones).

In a Desperate Position

The Amalekites had burned Ziklag and carried off all the women and children, among whom were David's wives, Ahinoam and Abigail. His men were so embittered they threatened to stone him. Six hundred angry soldiers with rocks could have made short work of David. The prospect was not a bright one. What to do? Panic would be the ordinary response. Then a frantic effort to escape, shift blame, vindicate himself, hide, talk his way out of a desperate position.

What did David do? He "sought strength in the Lord his God" (1 Sam. 30:6-7).

Simmer down. Kneel down. Be quiet for a few minutes when your own position looks desperate. If you haven't got a place to kneel or a minute for silence, send up an SOS for strength from the Lord your God. He is watching. His eye has taken in the whole situation, all that has happened and that now threatens to happen, and He has not run out of strength. Ask for it. He wants you to *ask*, wants your Declaration of Dependence.

Does such a prayer seem remote and impractical in the face of the fearful facts? It is the most practical thing you can do *first*. With God's strength come also His peace and His wisdom. Seek Him. Seek His strength. Seek and you will find. Don't seek and you won't find.

What Thanks Do We Expect?

M otives are pretty hard to track down—at least mine are. I imagine that I have accepted a task for the Lord—for His glory, for His service. Serving other people is serving the Lord. We know that much. But we won't have gotten well into the job before we discover that nobody is very impressed with what we are doing. Hardly anybody notices it, in fact, and nobody has suggested a round of applause. Perhaps we persist in the task, assuming that they'll "catch on," and take note.

Perhaps the only note they take is to criticize. Now what is our response?

"I have sincerely tried to do something for the Lord. Is *this* the kind of thanks I get?"

If we listen quietly perhaps the still, small voice will answer: What kind of thanks have *I* received? Have you forgotten the favor I showed you only yesterday? You are *My* servant. It is *My* work you are doing. Whose approval do you care about? Whose thanks are you looking for?

Answer those questions in the presence of God. We will then see the task in a new light.

No Visible Results?

S ometimes God told the prophets of old in advance that their prophesying would be futile. Nevertheless His orders stood: Speak to My people. Prophesy.

Man, your fellow-countrymen gather in groups and talk of you under walls and in doorways and say to one another, "Let us go and see what message there is from the Lord." So my people will come crowding in, as people do, and sit down in front of you. They will hear what you have to say, but they will not do it. "Fine words!" they will say, but their hearts are set on selfish gain. You are no more to them than a singer of fine songs with a lovely voice, or a clever harpist; they will listen to what you say but they will certainly not do it.

EZEKIEL 33:30-32

Are we to quit a task God has called us to do simply because people do not respond as we hope? Should we take visible results as the condition on which we persevere? Not by any means always. Let us be *faithful*. God give us the grace of continuance even when prospects are bleak, visible effects nil. *He* is at work behind the scenes, we are simply to do what He says—"as one who saw the invisible God" (Heb. 11:27).

O God, clear my vision. Help me to see with the eye of faith the things that can be seen in no other way.

A Short Bed

There will always be conditions in our lives which are not to our liking. "If only I had ... if only this ... if only he would ... etc." If our hearts are set on visible and temporal things we shall be irremediably miserable. It is a fractured world. But if we look up beyond the causes of our discontent to the invisible and the eternal we shall learn to be contented "with such things as we have" (Heb. 13:5), or, as we might say, with what we are "stuck with," assured that we have an "inheritance ... that nothing can destroy or spoil or wither ... kept for us in heaven" (1 Pet. 1:4).

"Whoever seeks the world to be their bed shall at best find it short and ill-made," wrote the young Samuel Rutherford.

Housecleaning

Every housewife knows what it is to have cleaned her house (she thought) quite thoroughly, and then to have an unexpected guest arrive. Suddenly the housewife notices places she missed —dust on a chair rung, fluff in the corners of a stair, spotted chrome on a faucet. She is looking now through the eyes of her visitor, which she imagines see everything.

So in the spiritual life it is easy to give what my mother called "a lick and a promise"—to clean just enough so that the family can live with it, with the intention of doing better next time. We allow ourselves a certain amount of imperfection and slovenliness. We are used to it, and our "house," we think, is "much cleaner than So-and-So's." To look at ourselves through the eyes of God—to inspect each corner with Him—will reveal much that must be put right.

"Examine me, O God, and know my thoughts. Test me, and understand my misgivings. Watch lest I follow any path that grieves thee; guide me in the ancient ways" (Ps. 139:23-24).

Cared for in the Wilderness

L ife holds for all of us, from time to time, desolate places. All that was ordinary and secure and familiar and dependable seems a thousand miles away. Here we are in this strange wilderness—out of work, ill, robbed of something or someone, banished from a privilege that once was ours, no longer needed, confused, forsaken. It is a place of dryness, loneliness, isolation, helplessness, fear. We feel as though we are walking where no human being was ever meant to walk, a place of *dragons.*

Don't despair. Even though you find no signs, be sure that thousands have traversed this terrain. When you reach the far side you will meet them. But there is something far more comforting than that. You are *not* alone *now.* Always beside you is Another whose voice you may not hear, whose arm you may not feel, whose footprint you may not see. Nevertheless His Word is utterly to be trusted:

"I cared for you in the wilderness, in a land of burning heat, as if you were in pasture" (Hos. 13:5-6).

Dear Shepherd, thank You for keeping this sheep in Your care.

Remember This in the Dark Place

When we ask God to work His holy will in us, we ought not to be surprised that the answer leads us sometimes into dark places. Where did it lead His Son? Whom do we follow?

Sorrow is at the very heart of things human. By taking on Himself human form, Jesus entered fully into our miseries and squalors, and presses us—if we love Him—to enter into the dark experience in order that we may share a little more in His Cross. We cannot know Him, and the power of His resurrection, if we seek to escape being *crucified with Him*. The end of God's story is joy—joy unspeakable and full of glory.

Lord, You well know how my flesh and my heart shrink from suffering, and how prone I am to forget that I once determined to follow One who was crucified. Yet in Your human flesh, dear Savior, You, too, shrank from the bitter cup Your Father offered. I humbly ask you to strengthen my weakness, forgive my hesitancy, and open my understanding that I may gladly receive the small share of pain which is mine. In Jesus' name.

This Is My Classroom

There is only one classroom in which to learn:
1. The work of God
2. The will of God
3. The trustworthiness of God
4. The presence of God

The classroom is where I am *now*. This is the place appointed by God for my instruction and sanctification—even here:

1. where it seems God is doing nothing (He *is*, in fact, at work in unseen ways);

2. where His will seems obscure or frightening (He will surely give me peace at last);

3. where He isn't doing what I want Him to (He is doing something better—preparing bread for me when what I asked was in actual fact a stone; or perhaps He is doing the very thing I prayed for, but in a way incomprehensible to me);

4. where He is most absent (yes, even there His promise holds: I will *never* leave you or forsake you. My faith must seize that written Word regardless of the enemy's taunt, "You've been abandoned.").

The Glory of Sacrifice

Do we think of sacrifice primarily as the giving up of something we shall miss very much, concentrating on our own self-deprivation and loss? Or can we see it rather as an *offering* to God of what is most precious to us—an offering that, as the Lord receives it into His hands and accepts it, is transformed into a glorious thing—into gain, not loss? How far are we to go in obedience? How much will it cost? If such questions frighten us, we are shortsighted. Let us look rather at Him whose face gave courage to Moses, who "was resolute, as one who saw the invisible God" (Heb. 11:27), or, as another translation has it, "he looked steadily at the ultimate, not the immediate, reward" (PHILLIPS). The offering is accepted, then turned into glory.

Perhaps today's offering is the letting go of a long-cherished hope; the health we have always enjoyed and counted on to continue; some pleasure, legitimate and natural, which we gladly forgo for the sake of someone else. These may all be offerings which, when made with a loving and peaceful heart may turn into undreamed-of blessing.

A Spiritual Conceit

The wish to accomplish "great" things for God often cloaks a reluctance to accept duty as our assigned ministry. Ordinary work is the usual place where we are meant to serve God, and if, in His providence, we are destined to do something extraordinary, it will be the reward of faithfulness in the ordinary. True saints do not recognize anything extraordinary in their own labors—they are "unprofitable" servants (Luke 17:10, KJV) and they know it. We miss the small gate which leads to life because we are looking for a majestic portal.

It is not an extraordinary spirituality that refuses to do ordinary work, but a disguised desire to demonstrate that we are "special"—in other words, it is a symptom of spiritual conceit.

Jesus Was Never Busy

To be busy is to be engaged in an occupation which makes it inconvenient to be disturbed." So wrote Janet Erskine Stuart, a woman with ceaseless demands on her time and strength, inasmuch as she was the Mother Superior of an English convent. She followed her Master in this. He was at the disposal of His Father at all times and therefore at the disposal of all whom the Father sent to Him. There was never a sign of moodiness, selfishness, offense, boredom, or busyness.

He never made a fuss about anything. This spirit of peace can be in us who are *in Him*. We can learn to see every minute of our day as His, not ours; every task to which we turn our attention as belonging to Him, not to us; everything that interrupts "our" work as His work which must take precedence. Knowing where we come from and to Whom we are going relieves us of the anxiety that makes us so fussy and so hard to live with.

Let your gentleness be evident to all. The Lord is near. Do not be anxious about anything, but in everything by prayer and petition, with thanksgiving, present your requests to God. And the peace of God, which transcends all understanding, will guard your hearts and your minds in Christ Jesus.

PHILIPPIANS 4:5-7, NIV

The Father's Answer

Remember Jesus in the Garden of Gethsemane. He dreaded what was to come to pass and prayed for deliverance. His prayer, however, was not the petulant demand of an angry child, but the humble petition of an obedient son: *Father, if You are willing.* Jesus did not want anything contrary to what His Father wanted. The "cup" was not removed. Escape was not granted. The second part of the prayer was granted: *Your will be done.*

And then "an angel from heaven appeared to Him and

strengthened Him" (Luke 22:43, NIV).

We may not be permitted to sidestep that thing we are dreading, but heaven will certainly send us all the help we need. When the Father's answer is No, let us not complain that He did not hear our prayer. No is an answer. His refusals are probably among His greatest acts of love—incomprehensible to us at the time, but after we have endured the trial, we will discover that we have been established, strengthened, and settled in a manner impossible had we not been given the chance (and the divine mercy) to endure.

Only a Child May Enter

Prayer, for some of us, does not seem to become easier, no matter how far we have traveled on the road of discipleship. It is hard work which calls for persistence, patience, and resolution, no matter how distracted and dull we may feel.

"Anyone who will not receive the Kingdom of God like a little child will not enter it" (Luke 18:17, NIV). Prayer is our daily entrance into that Kingdom—the uniting of ourselves to the will of God in a simple act of coming. The little child does not present his spirituality, his accomplishments, his religious history, his lofty feelings, or the purity of his motives or desires. He simply *comes*. Nothing to offer but himself. He does not *think* of offering anything in order to be received. He puts out his hand.

I put mine out to You, Lord. You have bade me welcome

and I have accepted. I bring mind, heart, and will to bear on the things I want to pray about. Please help me. Let me not give up in despair because I cannot *feel* that I am praying well. All my hope—feeble as it often is—is in You.

Lord, in Your mercy, hear my prayer.

No Question About the Supernatural

When Gabriel told Mary, "You will be with child and give birth to a son," she had a question about the natural: "How can this be ... since I am a virgin?" (Luke 1:31, 34, NIV)

When the answer was, "the Holy Spirit will come upon you and the Most High will overshadow you," she had no question about the supernatural. She was *satisfied* with God's answer. Her acceptance was immediate, her surrender complete.

Do you *understand* what is going on in the invisible realm of your life? Do you *see* how the visible things relate to a hidden Plan and Purpose? Probably not. Let it suffice you to know that God is there, always loving you with an everlasting love, always engineering a thousand things you have no idea of. Get on with your job. Go to sleep in peace. Trust Him.

When Things Come to Nothing

When God denies us the particular results we expected from our work, it is one of His mercies, for in this He purifies our souls from self-seeking. It is an opportunity for us to learn to make His glory our sole object.

"But this piece of work was meant for His glory." Even so, He knows better than we what best promotes that end. He is glorified in our trustful acceptance of His disposals, though no eye but His may see that act of faith. Perhaps it is for the eyes of the angels, too, and the great cloud of witnesses who watch us run the race that is set before us. Whatever glory God intends, we may rest in the sure confidence that when we pray for His will and His honor God knows exactly how to answer our prayer. What seems to us to have come to nothing the Lord knows how to turn into something. Leave it with Him.

The Long Leisure of Eternity

In Maud Monahan's *Life and Letters of Janet Erskine Stuart* (Maud Monahan, *Life and Letters of Janet Erskine Stuart* [London, New York, Toronto: Longmans Green & Co., 1922, 1953]), she describes the long years of waiting on God, and how He took nine years, "with all the long leisure of Eternity," to bring her to a Guide who would "lead her soul out into paths of confidence and joy."

That word helped me to see that some of what I would have called my own stalling and obtuseness may have been the Lord's own timing. He makes us *wait*. He keeps us on purpose in the dark. He makes us walk where we want to run, sit still when we want to walk, for He has things to do in our souls that we are not interested in.

There have been times, on the other hand, when He wanted me to run but I only walked. Let me remember, however, that the Shepherd Himself sometimes makes us to lie down. Some of the "delays" are His own choice for us, so we must not always chide ourselves when the pace is not what we thought it should be. We must learn to move according to the timetable of the Timeless One, and be at peace.

"My times are in Thy hand." That is where I want them to be, Father. May I rest in the sure knowledge that my hours and days are safely kept.

On Planks or Pieces of the Ship

When a boatload of prisoners, of whom the apostle Paul was one, was shipwrecked off the island of Malta, they might well have all been drowned. But God had sent His angel to stand beside Paul and to deliver His message of promise: Paul must stand trial before Caesar, and God would protect the lives of all who sailed with him. I imagine Paul would have been glad if God had arranged things so that he would be spared the trial.

If God could save everybody out of a disastrous storm at sea, He could have spared Paul his appearance in court, but He did not choose to.

He could have deposited them neatly on a sandy beach, but He did not choose to.

The ship ran aground, "the stern was broken to pieces by the pounding of the surf" (Acts 27:41, NIV), and the passengers had to swim ashore, or get themselves there, "on planks or on pieces of the ship" (v. 44). Such is often the divine deliverance: not exemption from trouble but *salvation*. We don't always "make it" to our goals as we had hoped, but God gets us there in *His* way.

Do Not Try to Save Yourself

It is our natural tendency to look out for ourselves first, last, and always. The soldier, on the other hand, fights for others, not for himself, and is therefore highly expendable. An army of men and women trained to save themselves would be of no use for saving a country.

Jesus calls us to a radical self-giving. It is not of any specially heroic variety most of the time, but radical nevertheless, in that it cuts the very roots of our selfishness. (Radical comes from a word meaning root, as does radish.)

If things go wrong, take responsibility—even blame—for them if you can and set about making them right.

Do not try to save yourself.

Do not explain too much.

Do not defend your position when what is needed is forward action.

If we keep our mouths shut and our eyes open, we can let God look after the business of saving us.

From moral weakness of spirit; from fear of men and dread of responsibility, strengthen us with courage to speak the truth in love and self-control; and alike from the weakness of hasty violence and moral cowardice, save us and help us, we humbly beseech Thee, O Lord.

> From *The Southwell Litany*
> *for the Personal Life*

Blessed Inconveniences

The trivial inconveniences of every day are not trivial in the spiritual life. They strike at the self-life, which gets in the way of selfless service. Meet them with goodwill and good humor. Welcome them as appointed by the Captain of our Salvation as "boot camp" training. If, after years of supposing that we are good soldiers, even officers in His army, we are bothered by the inconveniences, it is a sign that we are still in need of basic training. A college or seminary degree, a couple of summers on the mission field, a Bible school diploma cannot give any of us a joyful, devil-may-care response to inconvenience. That comes in *ordinary* life, in the acceptance of the most *mundane,* as matters designed and given by God for our perfection in holiness. The closer we come to holiness, the more clearly God's light shines through us.

Help me today, Lord, to recognize my inconveniences as blessed, and to grasp each as a chance to praise You.

All Things Serve Thee

I t ought to comfort rather than upset us when our own arrangements go awry—especially if we have prayed for guidance and the accomplishment of the will of God. The disruption of our own plans is sometimes the very means of God's working out His own—not that we have disobeyed or ignored His directions, but that He may assure us of His serene Providence. Our lives are in *His* hands, not our own. Our times are His, not ours. What looks to us like a serious disruption is fully under the control of Him who loved us and gave Himself for us, for, as the psalmist said, "All things serve thee" (Ps. 119:91). "The Lord works out everything for His own ends" (Prov. 16:4, NIV).

The Devil's Schemes

T he devil's schemes are many and very subtle, for he well knows how to approach us at the unguarded point. One of his schemes is to get us to argue about what God *doesn't* mean—for example, in the command: deny yourself and take up the Cross. Modern notions of prudence furnish us with inexhaustible material for this debate, and thus the enemy succeeds brilliantly in deflecting us from obedience, which is what he cares most about. He knows he can't change what's in the Book, but he can certainly prevent us from doing what it says.

Let it be our rule of life to start obeying, no matter how foolish it may seem. There will always be a struggle here, of course, because of the rulers, authorities, and powers of "this dark world," because of "spiritual forces of evil in the heavenly realms" (Eph 6:12, NIV), but the Lord with all His mighty power is on our side once we make up our minds to *do* the thing He says.

Truth, righteousness, peace, faith, salvation, and the Word of God are the armor that protects us. Prayer is the force against which the enemy has no power at all.

"Pray in the Spirit on all occasions, with all kinds of prayers and requests" (Eph 6:18, NIV).

Reason for Conflict

Whenever there is friction between two people, it is because there are hidden desires which have not been submitted to God. "You want something but don't get it. You kill and covet, but you cannot have what you want. You quarrel and fight. You do not have, because you do not ask God. When you ask, you do not receive, because you ask with wrong motives, that you may spend what you get on your pleasures" (James 4:2-3, NIV).

The desire may be for a good and legitimate thing, but it may not be in God's time or in God's way that we ask for it. In the case of a married couple, for example, each desires a perfect partner, a perfect relationship, and all failures, inadequacies, and imperfections are potential causes for conflict. When one wants something he doesn't get from the other, a battle begins—first in the heart, and spills over into criticism, which results in hurt feelings, retaliation ("and *you* haven't been meeting *my* needs either"), and quarreling.

If each made his hidden desires known first to God, and waited humbly and patiently for *His* answer (which may lie with the other), there would be peace.

Lord, help us to love. Give us Calvary love—a willingness to sacrifice.

A Simple Statement Suffices

Some of us feel thoroughly inadequate as "pray-ers." We wish we could pray beautifully and consistently and effectively, and we know we are not much good at it. But how "good" does one have to be to come to God? Take a look at these prayers:

"Lord, if you are willing, you can make me clean."

"Lord, my servant lies at home paralyzed and in terrible suffering."

"Lord, save us! We're going to drown!" (Matt. 8:2, 6, 25, NIV).

In each case the situation looked irremediable, but the petitioner recognized that there was One who might possibly do something about it. They saw the need. They saw their own helplessness. They saw the Lord. They made a simple statement to Him. That sufficed.

When Amy Carmichael found her cabin on shipboard infested with cockroaches she "went and told Jesus." Just such a little thing as placing a situation before Him has a calming effect. Then we can go on and do whatever the next thing may be.

Jesus says, "Come to Me. I will give you rest" (Matt. 11:28, NIV). What a foolish thing it is to hesitate on the ground that we don't know how to make fine prayers.

Nevertheless We Must Run Aground

Have you ever put heart and soul into something, prayed over it, worked at it with a good heart because you were sure it was what God wanted, and finally seen it "run aground"?

The story of Paul's voyage as a prisoner across the Adriatic Sea tells how an angel stood beside him and told him not to be afraid (in spite of a wind of hurricane force), for God would spare his life and the lives of all with him on board. Paul cheered his guards and fellow passengers with that word, but added, "Nevertheless, we must run aground on some island" (Acts 27:26, NIV).

It would seem that the God who promises to spare all hands

on board the ship might have "done the job right," saved the ship, and spared them the ignominy of reaching land "on planks or pieces of the ship" (v. 44). The fact is He did not, nor does He always spare us.

Heaven is not *here*, it's *there*. If we were given all we wanted here, our hearts would settle for this world rather than the next. God is forever drawing us up and away from this one, wooing us to Himself and His still invisible kingdom where we will certainly find what we so keenly long for.

Running aground on some island, then, is not the end of the world, but it helps to make the world a bit less appealing. It may even be God's answer to "Lead us not into temptation" (Matt. 6:13, NIV). Perhaps He saved them from a temptation which would have been too great for them.

God Tangles Himself in My Need

Our Father in Heaven is always at work in bringing to pass the lovely things His love has planned since before time began. But we work too—sometimes for and sometimes against His love. And therefore we find ourselves in great confusion. Even there, in the middle of a muddle, our holy Lord is calmly at work. But because He designed us according to a plan of personal freedom, we make choices, and many of them are wrong. We do not readily see that our truest freedom is to serve His will, and so, as George MacDonald says,

Thou therefore hast to work just like a man,
Tangling thyself in their sore need.

Diary of an Old Soul, July 5

It is reassuring to know that no disappointments will ever tire
His love for us—we have His promise: "He shall not fail nor
be discouraged" (Isa. 42:4, KJV).

Do you feel that you are hopelessly entangled in insoluble
problems? Nothing is insoluble to God. Look up. Pray. He is
in this thing somewhere.

Trust Him when dark doubts assail thee,
Trust Him when thy strength is small,
Trust Him when to simply trust Him
Seems the hardest thing of all.

Lucy A. Bennett

The Lifeline

Crowds of people came to hear Him and to be healed ...
but Jesus often withdrew" (Luke 5:15-16, NIV).

The earthly service of the Son of God included three
decades of silence before He did anything of which we are
allowed a record. Then in those three packed years of preach-
ing, teaching, and healing there was much silence. We learn of
His rising "a great while before day," of His going up into the
hills, of His taking His disciples away from the people for rest,
of His *often* withdrawing to lonely places so that He could
pray.

Prayer was His lifeline. What makes us think we can safely do without it, as though in "life's tempestuous sea" we need not bother to hold the rope thrown to us, but can make it without disaster on our own? In reading over some old journals I was distressed (and I hope soundly rebuked and instructed) to see here and there a pattern of prayerlessness and faithlessness. The two things went together. And where there is little faith there is little obedience. Where there is little prayer there is much spiritual confusion.

God help us, no matter how busy we may be, to *withdraw* from our business and our incessant busyness and pray. Without prayer we flounder.

Perseverance

T he reading of those old journals was an exercise in humiliation—because I find so much foolishness, selfishness, faithlessness, and pride. It is also an exercise in hope, for I can look away to my faithful Shepherd who loved me, gave Himself for me, and never forsook me. His mercy *is* everlasting. His faithfulness is great enough to reach me wherever I am. He has been dealing tenderly with me, guiding and teaching me, leading me closer to His Kingdom and to the image of His Son. He is never discouraged.

Jesus' parable of the sower ends with these words: "But the seed on good soil stands for those with a noble and good heart, who hear the word, retain it, and by *persevering* produce a crop" (Luke 8:15, NIV).

My heart, as revealed by many journal pages, seems anything but noble and good, yet there is also the evidence of God-hunger, the persistive longing to know and love and obey.

Do not give up on God because you're sure He must give up on *you!* Persevere. By perseverance (which is your part) and grace (which is His part) a crop will appear.

"Why should I start at the plough of my Lord, that maketh deep furrows on my soul? He is no idle husbandman, He purposeth a crop" (Samuel Rutherford).

Envy Blinds

"M orning by morning new mercies I see," we often sing. Is it the truth? One whose heart is grateful and humble and open toward the Father of Mercies sees them. But a heart that is drawn after things He has not given is blind to all the blessings. Envy closes our eyes to God's kindness.

Remember the story Nathan the prophet told David? A rich man who owned great flocks stole a poor man's one little beloved ewe lamb in order to feed a guest. David, outraged, said the man deserved death. Then the truth hit him: "Thou art the man" (see 2 Sam. 12:7). With all God had showered on him—kingship, deliverance from his enemy Saul, and a whole string of wives, David stole Uriah's only wife and arranged for the murder of Uriah. God said he had *despised* Him (see 2 Sam. 12:10).

Here is my heart, Lord God, thankful for a thousand

mercies, not only the new ones I see today but all the old ones. (Here we might list a few dozen or so.) Forgive my blindness whereby I have focused on what I have envied. Sweep out the discontent. Give me a merry, humble, ever-thankful heart that honors You.

Creative Love

How much faith does it take to believe in God? Less, I venture to say—a great deal less—than to believe in "the Un-conscious generating the Conscious."

"Mindlessness creating Mind."

"Nothing giving birth to Something."

What we know of God we have seen in His Son. He in whom we are asked to trust is Love, creative Love, thinking of us before He thought of stars, giving Himself in sacrificial love before He gave us His own breath.

My Lord and my God—I believe. Stabilize my faith, strengthen me to stand.

The Exceptional Case

The one Jesus called the Father of Lies has a vast assortment of tricks. One of them is to convince us that our case is exceptional. "The Word says so-and-so, but it won't work in *my* situation." That attitude accepts the lie and makes a liar of God. Better far to come to Him who is truth, present the Word and the "exceptional" case, and ask Him to show us what to do. This was the psalmist's prayer:

"Thy hands moulded me and made me what I am; show me how I may learn thy commandments. Let all who fear thee be glad when they see me, because I hope for the fulfillment of thy word" (Ps. 119:73-74).

The Acceptance of Suffering

The natural tendency of all of us humans is to accept self and deny suffering. We say yes to ourselves, no to the Cross. But this simply will not do if we have any idea of becoming real disciples. The mystery of suffering touches the deepest place in our hearts where we may meet God. If we refuse it, we close the door to Him, to the possibility of purification and revelation. We must turn completely around, do the thing most unnatural—with supernatural help—and say yes to the Cross and all that it means of self-denial and acceptance of pain, loss, humiliation, death. The vistas of light and glory that will open to us if we will pay this steep price are unimaginable. But of course we may have to wait a long time. Today we are faced with the choice.

> O Prince of Glory, Who dost bring
> Thy sons to glory through the Cross,
> Let us not shrink from suffering,
> Reproach, or loss.
>
> Amy Carmichael, *Toward Jerusalem*

Stripped

Jesus was not only crucified, He was first stripped. But long before He was subjected to either of those unspeakable outrages, He stripped Himself: In willing and utter acceptance of the mind and will of the Father whom He loved He had laid down everything—all that He *was* in Heaven, all that He *had*. Nobody could take more from Him than He had already given.

We say we are His followers. Do we speak the truth? We meant to—but we did not know what it would entail.

"Will you deny yourself?" He asks.

"Well, yes, Lord—up to a point."

"Will you take up your cross?"

"Yes, if it's *this* one You mean. I'm not sure I'd want to take up *that* one."

"Will you follow Me?"

"I think I will, Lord. How far are You going? Dear Lord, enable me to go all the way with You, for Your glory."

Glory in Common Things

No matter how far along our spiritual pilgrimage we may have come, we need to be shown time after time that humble, ordinary things can be very holy, very full of God. We may hope for visions and revelations and wonderful experiences, forgetting that the context of the revelation of God to each one of us is *exactly where we are*—here, on earth, in this house, this room, this work, this family, this physical body.

Think of the revelation of the divine life to the Bethlehem shepherds: the sudden appearance of the angel of the Lord and the glory of the Lord, the song of high praise sung by the "multitude of the heavenly host"—certainly a most wonderful experience—but it came while they were faithfully doing their usual job, just where they belonged.

And think of this—how did the divine life come to Mary? While angels were singing for the shepherds, she was sweating and straining in the darkness and discomfort of a stable. Reality was being given to her through agony and blood. Her mind could hardly have been filled during those painful hours with pure exulting. It was a *baby*, a human baby, helpless and squalling, that she must attend to. She was the "handmaid of the Lord," carrying out her task in pain and squalor, neither seeing (so far as we know) the glory of the Lord nor hearing the angels' song.

> So God imparts to human hearts
> The blessings of His heaven.
>
> "O Little Town of Bethlehem"
> Phillips Brooks

Stress, Discipline, and Choice

Three elements are essential to spiritual growth: stress, discipline, and choice. Have any of you experienced any of these lately?

We see them at the outset of Jesus' ministry—first He went ("was led") into the wilderness, a place of hardship and loneliness, in other words, stress. There He fasted—a severe discipline. Then He was confronted by temptation, which necessitated clear-cut choices.

If this was the divine pattern for the Son of Man, so it must be for all who follow Him. (Does this surprise us?) Usually we recognize great stress when it comes, but often we are unprepared to see the importance of those unexpected smaller forms which we encounter nearly every day, things like someone's hurtful remark, a traffic jam which delays us, a broken appliance, an interruption or inconvenience of any kind—things that require a *response*. The response reveals the character and is a practice session for greater stresses later on.

Our "wilderness" may be one of perplexity, perhaps in a very little decision, but this is an occasion for spiritual growth if we bring to it the discipline of prayer and the refusal to be anxious as we make our choice. Stress, discipline, choice. Do you see what I mean?

When the Tempter came to Jesus in the wilderness with his master-strokes, he met a man well trained to discern His duty. Years of discipline in a carpenter shop had borne the fruit of spiritual maturity. No peculiarly "spiritual" environment had been provided for the learning of these lessons. His home, His family life, His work in the shop (we suppose) furnished the perfect conditions where He learned obedience. What sort of conditions are yours?

> He said unto them ... "Lacked ye any thing?" And they said, "Nothing."
>
> LUKE 22:35, KJV

Let God Choose the Curriculum

There is one school of thought which holds that the student ought to be allowed to assemble his own curriculum solely according to his preferences. One can't help wondering what basis the student has for making such choices. His idea of what he needs to learn is not only greatly limited but also greatly distorted. What he needs is *help*—from those who know much more than he does.

The teacher's task of choosing curriculum is a hard one, but she is better equipped to do it than her pupils.

Our Father's wisdom is perfect, His knowledge all-embracing—not only of what the world contains but of what each of His loved children needs to learn. With intimate understanding of our deepest needs and of our individual capacities He chooses our curriculum. We need only ask, "Give us *this* day our daily bread, our daily lessons, our homework." We can count on Him to hear that prayer. Can He count on us to apply ourselves to His curriculum?

Lord, send out Thy light and Thy truth. Let them lead me. Help me to follow.

How to Prepare to Hear God

Preparation is needed before we can receive the deepest of divine lessons. The Holy Spirit works in us, but we must cooperate with Him. When difficult things happen we are tempted to think of God as *against* us—He seems to become what He became for Job, the adversary. But of course that is wildly untrue, and when He (with great grace and patience) brings us to our senses we can begin the lesson by thanking Him.

Through thanksgiving we deliberately acknowledge our dependence and debt to Him, our Maker and our always-loving Father. He is *not* against us, He is *for* us, and "if God be for us, who can be against us?" (Rom. 8:31, KJV) So we surrender our resentments and take our place in humble gratitude at His feet. We do not understand the lesson yet, but thanking Him, we come with open heart and mind to be taught. Thanksgiving, then, opens the heart, and readies it for His entrance.

"He who sacrifices thank offerings honors me, and he prepares the way so that I may show him the salvation of God" (Ps. 50:23, NIV).

Hurt Yet Peaceful

A careless look or tone of voice can light a fuse of anger in another, who then burns us with hot words. Has it happened to you lately? It happened to me. I ran to God with the words still burning in my ears, and prayed:

"Teach me to treat all that comes to me with peace of soul and with firm conviction that Your will governs all."

Where could that kind of peace come from? Only from God, who gives "not as the world gives."

His will that I should be burned? Not exactly, but His will *governs* all. In a wrong-filled world we suffer (and cause) many a wrong. God is there to heal and comfort and forgive, and this thing occurred with His full knowledge and permission. He means it for my ultimate blessing, and, I think, even for an increase in love between me and the one who hurt me.

"The one who feeds on Me will live because of Me" (John 6:57, NIV).

The Work of God Displayed

R abbi," the disciples said to Jesus, "who sinned, this man or his parents, that he was born blind?"

"Neither this man nor his parents sinned," said Jesus, "but this happened so that the work of God might be displayed in his life" (John 9:2-3, NIV).

Jesus then healed the man, and so the work of God was seen by all. Miracles drew crowds then as now, but the work of God is not limited to what we call miracles. Sometimes He needs to display the work of grace in a human life—the hour by hour, day by day, week by week demonstration of trust, as in the case of Job; of supernatural strength made perfect in weakness, as in the case of Paul; of joy in the midst of suffering, as in the case of the exiles to whom Peter wrote his letters.

God might choose to lift you straight out of a painful situation today, and thus display His work in a way you could shout about. Or His choice—to give you grace to trust, power in weakness, joy in pain—might be a greater display of His work.

Choose for us, God, not let our weak preferring
Cheat us of good Thou hast for us designed.
Choose for us God—Thy wisdom is unerring,
And we are fools and blind.

W.H. Burleigh

The Facets of Redemption

When Jesus accepted the will of the Father He accepted the radical weakness of human nature—an utter stripping and abandonment. "He poured out His soul unto death" (Isa. 53:12, NIV). When He rose from the grave, He was filled with power—that omnipotence which is the Life of God. This immolation and glory are the two great elements of our salvation, and we may not receive salvation without receiving death and resurrection. It is a radical surrender in humility—"I am crucified"—and a radical rising in power and newness of life—"not I, but Christ liveth in me" (Gal. 2:20, KJV).

Salvation consists in the total welcome given by weakness to glory.

Each fresh experience that requires a voluntary laying down of my will (when, for example, someone else's will crosses mine, someone else is preferred before me, someone else's convenience means my inconvenience) is my chance to *welcome glory*—to say, "Come in, Lord Jesus. Rule in my heart."

And so I am being redeemed, being saved, being changed from glory to glory.

Self-Disgust

"I n the world you will have trouble," Jesus warned us. "But courage! The victory is mine; I have conquered the world" (John 16:33).

Perhaps the hardest kind of tribulation for us to endure is that which we have brought on ourselves. It is hard to endure because it hurts our pride—we have been stupid or thoughtless or downright deliberately sinful (and who of us can claim never *knowingly* to have done wrong?) We flagellate ourselves instead of running at once to our Savior. We sweat and stew in self-disgust until the thing becomes an intolerable burden, when all along the Lord wants to rid us of it more than we want to be rid of it. Do we doubt the possibility of forgiveness just because "we knew better"?

No matter how intolerable we are to ourselves and how inexcusable the fault, the antidote is exactly the same as always: the blood of Jesus. Be of good cheer! He has overcome the world in *all* its forms, in *all* its power, and He has nothing to do but to save us. This is what He loves to do. For "Christ loved the Church and gave Himself up for her to make her holy" (Eph. 5:25-26). Can He give up that purpose before it is fully accomplished?

Confess your sin. Confess its deliberateness—that, too, the Blood will cover. Stop stewing. Leave your pride at the Cross. Christ still loves you. *Christ* will make you holy.

The Holy Paradox

Jesus asked the Father that the cup might pass from Him, but added, "Yet it must not be what I want, but what You want" (Matt. 26:39, PHILLIPS).

Twice after praying He found the disciples (whom He had asked to stay awake with Him) sleeping.

"Are you still going to sleep and take your ease?" He asked. "In a moment you will see the Son of Man betrayed into the hands of evil men. Wake up, let us be going!" (Matt. 26:46, PHILLIPS).

Jesus' prayer was for whatever God *wanted*. How could God *want* His beloved Son to be betrayed into the hands of evil men? We know the answer—because He had the salvation of the world in mind. Yet the answer is still fraught with mystery—salvation through a terrible evil. And still He works His holy will through holy paradoxes.

Let us try to focus on this one, of all the mysteries that stretch our faith almost to the breaking point—the anguished Son of Man kneeling in the garden, a loving Father hearing His prayer, while evil men are on their way to capture Him. There would be suffering—unspeakable suffering and death— but God knew there would be glory. There would be a resurrection and an ascension.

Lord, help us, in our sorrows and pain, to stay our souls on the promise of glory.

"Now if we are children, then we are heirs—heirs of God and co-heirs with Christ, if indeed we share in his sufferings in order that we may also share in his glory. I consider that our present sufferings are not worth comparing with the glory that will be revealed in us" (Rom. 8:17-18, NIV).

His Peace and Ours

The Pharisees resented Jesus' having healed a man on the Sabbath. This was against Jewish law. They resented even more His unanswerable questions which put them firmly in their place: "Is it right to do good on the Sabbath day, or to do harm? Is it right to save life or to kill?" (Mark 3:4, PHILLIPS). The best thing to do with such a man, the Pharisees decided, was to kill Him.

Jesus did not argue. He did not panic. He "retired to the lakeside with his disciples" (Luke 3:7, PHILLIPS).

His peaceful assurance that His Father was in control enabled Him in every situation to face the truth, to respond with wisdom given to Him by His Father, and to go on to do the next thing undisturbed.

Such also will be *our* peace—an unwavering trust in God's watchful care and a calm obedience.

Proof of the Fear of the Lord

The fear of God is the giving over to Him all that we are and have because He is perfectly trustworthy. Peter says we are to "live your lives as strangers here in reverent fear" (1 Pet. 1:17, NIV). Recognizing who God is inspires both fear and trust, for He is both my *judge* and my *savior*.

Even in earliest times, long before the perfect revelation of God's love at Calvary, one man proved both his fear and trust when he offered up the most precious thing in his life.

Abraham had raised the knife to kill his son when the angel of the Lord told him not to lay a hand on the boy. "Now I know that you fear God because you have not withheld from me your son, your only son" (Gen. 22:12, NIV). An unconditional surrender was not a capitulation or defeat, alone. It was, for all the ages to come, a demonstration that the true fear of God goes hand in hand with trust.

"Abraham reasoned that God could raise the dead" (Heb. 11:19, NIV).

Teach me, Lord, to fear You reverently and to trust You utterly. May I never fear You without trust or trust You without fear.

My Work—or His?

There is greed in my piling work on work, and constant fretting that I cannot do more. My memory is overloaded, and much spills out. Am I the builder of my life, or is God? Am I to be born of God, or only of man? Will I let Him shape me to *His* image, or am I too busy shaping my own?

Lord, let all hurry and bustle vanish as I surrender to Your peace. Help me to take up my work with gladness, confident of Your promise to work *in* me to will and do of Your good pleasure.

"Strive to be as a little child who, while its mother holds its hand, goes on fearlessly, and is not disturbed because it stumbles and trips in its weakness" (St. Francis de Sales).

The Long Way Around

The ways of God are often incomprehensible to us. He does not act according to our concepts of economy and efficiency because He knows the end from the beginning. Why would He say no to a prayer for a "speedy" recovery? Why would He allow us to make mistakes that cost time and money? Why should work faithfully done end in futility?

We have one clue in Exodus 13:17-18. God took the people of Israel the long way around by the desert toward the Red Sea because He knew that temptation lay on the short route: "The people may change their minds when they see war before them, and turn back to Egypt."

God is interested in our being made into His image—holy, perfect, glorious. There is no inefficiency or waste in His methods. How often in His mercy, unappreciated by us, He leads us *not* into temptation but away from it, for He has promised never to allow us to be tempted beyond our powers of endurance.

He Knows the Truth

Have you come suddenly into a collision with someone who is hurt by it and there is nothing on earth you can do or say that will help? When any attempt to explain or soothe will appear to be nothing better than self-defense? Be content, then, to refer all to Him who alone can save and heal and restore. Be content to follow Him who opened not His mouth. Be content in that silence. He knows the truth of the thing, and will one day bring forth His righteousness as the light and His judgment as the noonday. Shut your mouth and open your heart—He will heal *your* heart too.

Not My Prerogative

It is not my prerogative to determine the scope of my influence, or the limits of my service. I am the property of the Lord of the Universe. He raises one and puts down another. "He chose our inheritance for us" (Ps. 47:4, NIV). It is a perfect choice, perfectly fitted to His inscrutable purposes and to my individual need.

Like a master stonemason, He shapes the stone exactly to fit the place where He means it to go. The choice of its place, the weight it is to bear, its size and shape, its surface (rough or smooth), and the tools He must employ for its preparation are *not* the prerogatives of the stone. They are the prerogatives of the Master.

Jesus, the Cornerstone, took His place in an unconditional surrender to His Father's appointment.

This We Know

Those who love God know Him—are rather in the process of knowing Him as they learn to take Him at His word. Those who are unsure of their God demand *proofs*. "We must see with our eyes, hear with our ears—then we can believe."

God's order is the reverse. He gives us His Word. Therefore we know. We know that He loves us—the Bible tells us so. We know that all things work together for good to them that love

God. Seldom do we *see* that working together. The promised good is often hidden from our eyes, that we may lay hold of the promise by faith, and thus *know* it is true. In the divinely appointed time we shall *see*, but unless we trust the Lord we shall be like the Pharisees, of whom Jesus said, "You will be ever seeing but never perceiving" (Matt. 13:14, NIV).

In the barren places of my life I can be assured that God is there as He is when life is fruitful, and that the time is coming (Give me patience, Lord, to wait!) when He will fulfill His Word:

"I will plant cedars in the wastes, and acacia and myrtle and wild olive; the pine shall grow on the barren heath side by side with fir and box, that men may see and know, may once for all give heed and understand that the Lord himself has done this" (Isa. 41:19-20).

Like little children on Christmas Eve, we *know* that lovely surprises await us. Tomorrow we shall *see*.

Bad Moods

To permit ourselves the luxury of indulging in a bad mood opens the door to self-deception. My selfishness appears to be quite right, quite justifiable, and I am offended that others oppose me in this. A bad mood closes the door to the feelings of others, adversely affects the climate of the home (or wherever I happen to be), and makes me unapproachable.

Is it *my* self that is ruler of my life or is it the Christ-self, He who lives in me and desires to manifest His life through me? The moment I become aware of my evil mood, I must "push it rough aside," as George MacDonald says, "and hold obedient course" (*Diary of an Old Soul,* Feb. 2).

No bad language must pass your lips, but only what is good and helpful to the occasion, so that it brings a blessing to those who hear it. And do not grieve the Holy Spirit of God, for that Spirit is the seal with which you were marked for the day of our final liberation. Have done with spite and passion, all angry shouting and cursing, and bad feeling of every kind. Be generous to one another, tender-hearted, forgiving one another as God in Christ forgave you.

EPHESIANS 4:29-32

Forgiveness Is an Act of Faith

I won't forgive him until I can mean the words," a woman said to me of her husband, at whose hands she had suffered a good deal.

What did she mean? That when she "got over it" she would be ready to forgive? That she was going to wait until she "felt good" about him, or felt inclined to forgive? Was she hoping that the man might do good deeds sufficient to outweigh the evil he had done to her—and would thus "deserve" to be forgiven?

None of the above will work. Forgiveness is a decision to move toward Christ. He calls us to forgive, and no matter how great the sin committed, no matter how bitterly we have been hurt or how devastating the effects of the sin on ourselves or on those we love, we must simply move on the basis of His Word alone. That is the act of faith that is required of Christians. We are not asked to predict and provide for the consequences of this kind of action. We must lay aside all fear of results, all proud insistence on apologies, all human arguments about what "good" or what "harm" may come of it, and in true meekness, by the grace of God, *do* it. Forgive—freely, fully, and forever, as God for Christ's sake has forgiven us.

The Weapon of Forgiveness

The one who is truly humble is utterly vulnerable—and his humility and vulnerability make him, in reality, invulnerable. No one can hurt him in any way for which he cannot "retaliate"—the irresistible weapon of retaliation is forgiveness. Who can have the "last word," who can fling the final retort, who can cast the last stone, if he has already been forgiven? The one who forgives stands fully protected in the whole armor of God, helmet, shield, sword, breastplate furnished by God's grace. He fights as his Captain fought—by silence, by patience, by love, freely forgiving, freely receiving any injury, any insult, any attack that can come from any quarter, in the strength of Jesus Christ who *poured out his soul to death.*

He was despised ... tormented
And humbled by suffering;....
pierced for our transgressions,
tortured for our iniquities....
He *submitted* to be struck down....
Without protection, without justice,
he was taken away:...
stricken to the death...
made himself a sacrifice for sin.

ISAIAH 53:3, 5, 7, 8, 10

To the man or woman prepared to follow the Master to this degree, nobody can do anything. He is the conqueror—he is *more than* conqueror through Him that loved us!

How to Help People

When Thou tookest upon Thee to deliver man, Thou didst humble Thyself..."

The words of the *Te Deum* from the Book of Common Prayer give us the key to helping people. The deeper the trouble one is in, the farther down must go the one who is to "save" him.

Christ took it upon Himself to rescue us from death itself—death which came into the world only because man sinned. In order, then, to reach us, He had to be willing to go down, not only into our dark world, not only into our human flesh, but into death itself, the last horror, to face the last enemy.

We are tempted to take pride in being "counselors" to those who are in trouble. We shall never release them from their bondage unless we are willing to live the life of Christ and die the death of Christ—that is, to humble ourselves, to suffer for them and with them, take blame, be offended, "make ourselves nothing" (Phil. 2:7).

The Fear of Loss

Selfishness takes many forms. The fear of loss is one of them. It leads to sin against others when we are concerned with "saving our own skin." Think, for example, of the fear of losing:

1. reputation
2. opportunity for advancement
3. credit
4. recognition
5. position
6. beauty
7. youth
8. health
9. money
10. the love of friends or children
11. compliments
12. popularity
13. security
14. privacy
15. "rights"
16. people you love
17. job
18. home
19. dreams
20. power

Consider each of these separately, noting what sort of sin each kind of loss might tempt you to commit, noting also what kind of faith will be required to commit such a fear to God. *Has* He, in fact, made provision for these things? The list is not a list of sins. It is a list of quite legitimate benefits, often pure gifts from God. But to grasp them selfishly and greedily, to hang on to them fiercely, and to allow yourself to live in the fear of losing them is to deny Christ. It is to deny the power of the resurrection.

Guilt

A lady told me yesterday that she has suffered from terrible guilt ever since she put her mother in a nursing home six months ago. What should she do?

There is only one remedy for guilt: the blood of Christ. But first she needs to determine whether she has sinned in placing her mother there. If so, she must confess it, to God and to her mother. Then the thing to do is to get her out of the home. If, on the other hand, she has not sinned, she must commit those feelings (for they are mere feelings) of guilt to God, and *leave* the results of her decision in His hands.

The enemy delights in holding us captive by imaginary guilt, or by persuading us that real guilt persists when in fact it has been dealt with. But He who is in us is greater.

> He breaks the power of cancelled sin.
> He sets the prisoner free.
> His blood can make the foulest clean—
> His blood availed for me.
>
> "O For a Thousand Tongues to Sing"
> Charles Wesley

Tradition

Custom, ceremony, and tradition have fallen on hard times. There is a tendency to dispense with the tried-and-proven ways of doing things and to innovate. We look for spontaneity, newness, the "unstructured," sometimes thinking that we are on Jesus' side by so doing, for did He not condemn the Pharisees for clinging to tradition? It was their clinging to tradition to the point of putting aside the commandments of God that He condemned. If the plate has more importance than the Bread of Life, they have absolutized the minutiae of the law. This deserved the Lord's condemnation.

On the other hand, let us not dismiss wise custom simply because it is custom. Very likely it is the *best* way of doing a thing. This is precisely why it has become customary. Otherwise it would not have survived.

Lord, may we humbly learn from the wisdom of others, not presuming to have our own way for the sake of "originality," but keep us, Lord, from insulating ourselves from the Bread of Life by mere tradition.

Instant Obedience

With my own hands I founded the earth, with my right hand I formed the expanse of sky; when I summoned them they sprang at once into being.... If only you had listened to my commands" (Isa. 48:13, 18).

Take a look at the sky some night, pierced with stars; at the bright glory of a springtime sunrise; at great rolling thunderheads carrying a storm. Who called them into being? Look at the earth—glorious, tender, prodigious, sweet. Whose design was it? There was no reluctance there, ever. God spoke—it sprang at once to view.

But we drag our heels. We're not sure God can be trusted. We ask, "What *is* this He's asking? What does He have in mind? Where is He taking me?" We come to a dead halt and question our feelings, examine our ability to do the thing or our inclination to comply. To *comply!* With the Lord of the Universe! The King of Kings, Lord of Lords, the Ancient of Days!

"If only you had listened to my commands. Your prosperity would have rolled on like a river in flood and your just success like the waves of the sea" (Isa. 48:18).

God, deliver me from meanness and narrowness of heart, from playing in trickles and puddles, rather than giving myself fully and at once to the power of Your floods and oceans.

Lord, let my love for You be of the kind that, hearing Your word of command, springs at once to obedient action.

198 / Elisabeth Elliot

Let God Rescue Him

Never be troubled or surprised when it seems as though God is deaf or absent. Those times when you most need Him and expect a dramatic deliverance are the times when He may test your faith. The will, too, will test you by whispering, "So you trust God? Let God rescue you *now!*" It is not a new question. It is precisely the one hurled at Jesus when He was pinned helpless to the Cross. It was, in fact, the religious leaders—chief priests, lawyers, and elders—who threw out the atheistic challenge, "Let Him come down now from the cross and then we will believe Him" (Matt. 27:42). This is the frame of a worldly mind: *if* God does so-and-so, I'll trust Him, if He doesn't, I won't. Real faith trusts absolutely. Real faith is a willed choice, made in the very teeth of adversity.

"Though war were waged against me, my trust would still be firm" (Ps. 27:3, JB).

God's Arm—Too Short?

When we are faced with a task not to our liking, it is much easier to complain about it and put off the doing of it than it is to pray about it and buckle down to business. What an awful waste of time it is to discuss it with everybody but God! It is as if we have already decided that the thing can't be done, so why bother God? What's He got to do with it? This was my attitude this morning. The task was a piece of writing. I was stewing inwardly and evading the job when the Lord, through the morning's Scripture passage, said, "Did you think my arm too short to redeem. Did you think I had no power to save?" (Isa. 50:2).

Well, of course, Lord—You can *redeem* and You can *save,* but I'm not quite sure You can simply help me.

"The Lord God stands by to help me" was the next word. Get busy. He will not do the job for you. You must do it, but His arm, His power—strong to redeem, mighty to save—will enable you.

Burning and Tender Love

Because we ourselves are so hard on the sins of others and so soft on our own, because we are so prone to attribute to God the feelings and actions we would like Him to have, it is a good thing to read chapters like Isaiah 63. This brings into balance the character of the fierce, holy God who loves us and who Himself pays the terrible price of pure love. We cannot read that chapter and sentimentalize His love. It speaks of His clothes, red with the blood of those who reject Him, of His might, His rage and fury, His vengeance. Immediately Isaiah then turns to the Lord's acts of unfailing love, His great goodness, tenderness, pity—how He Himself delivered Israel—not an envoy, not an angel, but the Lord Himself "lifted them up and carried them through all the years gone by" (v.9).

Like us, Israel rebelled. What a dangerous business rebellion is against such a God, what risks we take, with what arrogance! Then the prophet asks, "Where is thy burning and tender love?"

O Lord, help me today to answer Your tender love in adoration and obedience. Cleanse me of all rebellion, every high thought that exalts itself against You. Let Your burning love make me pure for Jesus' sake.

Better to Be Maimed

Some of the words that came from the lips of Jesus are words of fire. They are anything but "comfortable words." Take these: "If your hand or your foot is your undoing, cut it off and fling it away; it is better for you to enter into life maimed ... than to keep two hands or two feet and be thrown into the eternal fire" (Matt. 18:8).

Mere "common sense" tells us we must keep our own lives (our bodies, plans, lifestyles, programs, possessions) *intact*. We "owe it to ourselves" not to put up with people who threaten to undo us. We ought not to risk personal loss and suffering if there is any way to get out of it. Get out of it? But what if we are more interested in *getting in* to the Kingdom of God? It may well be, in that case, that it will take some actual maiming, some deliberate renunciation of a perfectly good thing—even if it is something God wanted us to have.

How much is it worth to me today, Lord, to follow You? Help me to pay the price gladly and at once. Help me to hold Your gifts on an open palm.

Both Hands, Both Feet, Both Eyes

We have a God-given "right"—according to His original design—to hands, feet, and eyes, two of each. They are good things to have, very necessary things, but they also provide the potential for destruction if wrongly used. They can send us to hell. Standing on our rights may very well be for us the direct route to hell. That is where we would all be if Jesus had done that. He let go all of them—laid down His rights in order to take up our wrongs; gave hands and feet to the iron nails, His whole holy body not just to maiming, but to death. He was undone, "flung away," discarded. He descended *into* Hell in order to save us *from* Hell. It was what Love required. Because He was willing to be given over to death, we enter into life.

Lord, today I offer to You all my body—both hands, both feet, both eyes, heart, mind, and soul. Do as You want with any of it, take all of it, only make me fit to come into Your Kingdom. I praise You, Jesus, for receiving me with such love.

Take the Word to Heart

When the plague of hail was sent on Pharaoh those who "feared the word of the Lord" hustled slaves and cattle under cover. But those who did not take to heart the word of the Lord left them in the open. The Word is original and it is final. To obey it means life. To disobey it means death. There is no neutral ground.

The Word was in the beginning. The Word was *God*.

Every time we open the Bible we should expect something vital to be given to us and something to be required of us. It is very powerful and very dangerous, rather like radiation in that if the rays enter the body ("are taken to heart") they will burn and kill, but they will also (sometimes) heal. The Word of the Lord will pierce and burn and slay, but it will also (unlike radiation, it can be depended upon to) give us life. But we must be willing to allow its entrance—we must take it to heart.

Topic Index

4-21-01

Love always means sacrifice.
- Oblation - we have so much fun, so
many things, time - an oblation is a
giving over of these things to God - totally.
  Corrie Ten Boom - prison - sang for joy - every morn.
  Amy Carmichael - India (childrens ministry).
Mary - behold (me) the handmaiden of the
Lord. ♪ It is well with my soul. ♪
Christ - no my but thy will be done.
        What have I done with my years?
        what is He doing now.

Ecuadore 1952 - tribal languages
She had linguistic training.
  Colorados - painted themselves
colorful. 1st Peter (ashes) 4:12
man - Spanish + Colorado murdered.
Her work confiscated. Jim Elliot came
over asked her to marry him - had to
learn Quichua. all his yearly work
down the Amazon in a flood. Why?
God? Does God explain Himself? No it
is because He is shaping us in the
image of His son.
                              (poured out)
1. Sacrements of the will of God. (poured out)
2. Obedience - Jesus says I love the
Father and I will do exactally what He
asks.
        (by his appt.)   (strange? confided?)
  1. God brought me here (strange? confided?)
  2. He will keep me here in his
  love & give me grace.
      (In His Keeping.)

3. He will make my trial a blessing.
(under his training.)
4. In His good time He can bring
me out again.
(Luke 19:40) (In His timing.)

Were you placed here by God for
fun? It is an oblation - a
glad giving up of myself,
my plans.

It is good to submit, every
creature we lean upon should fail
us. To keep us humble and
prayerful. all these things go to
sowing in tears. Heb 10:14.
This is a process of being made
holy. take one day at a time.
We don't want to be poured out, or
irritated even.
Accustom yourself to unreasonableness
and mistreatment. Abide in peace
in the presence of God. Be content
doing w/calmness what God has
for me.
3. For the joy. - The weaver (poem)
Heb 12 (Let us throw off the encumbrance

Jesus - For the joy set before
Him. Purest form of worship. Everything is worship, if it is for Him.
    Jesus learned obedience through
the things He suffered - The creater of
the universe was a man.
    My life is a daily present -
We give to the Lord. Everything
we do should be offered up
to the Lord. Laundry is a service
of worship. Her second husband
was bedridden - she offers her own
life. She cared for him.
    Example - rich lady carrying
mops + toilet paper, for Jesus
Christ. Thank God Betty He
allowed me to carry mops +
toilet paper.